# THE AKASHIC RECORDS

*To your past, present and future self.*

First published in Great Britain in 2025
by Godsfield Press, an imprint of
Octopus Publishing Group Ltd
Carmelite House
50 Victoria Embankment
London EC4Y 0DZ
www.octopusbooks.co.uk
www.octopusbooksusa.com

An Hachette UK Company
www.hachette.co.uk

The authorized representative in
the EEA is Hachette Ireland,
8 Castlecourt Centre,
Dublin 15, D15 XTP3, Ireland
email: info@hbgi.ie



Distributed in the US by
Hachette Book Group
1290 Avenue of the Americas,
4th and 5th Floors
New York, NY 10104

Distributed in Canada by
Canadian Manda Group
664 Annette St., Toronto,
Ontario, Canada M6S 2C8



ISBN 978-1-84181-614-2

A CIP catalogue record for this book is available from the British Library.

Printed and bound in Dubai.

10 9 8 7 6 5 4 3 2 1

**Commissioning Editor:** Louisa Johnson
**Senior Editor:** Alex Stetter
**Art Director:** Jaz Bahra
**Designer:** Megan van Staden
**Deputy Picture Manager:** Jennifer Veall
**Assistant Production Manager:** Lisa Pinnell

MIX
Paper | Supporting responsible forestry
FSC
www.fsc.org
FSC® C004800

**Picture Acknowledgements**
Alamy Stock Photo: Artokoloro/Penta Springs Limited 31, bjphotographs 149br; Dreamstime.com: Andreykuzmin 32, Biljanacvetanovic 58, Elenabsl 92; Courtesy Earthly Gems, earthlygems.com 146 right; iStock: Anastasiia_M 45, Arina Gladyisheva 4, 30, 63, 91, 192, Bitter 103, BruceBlock 145r, Bwiselizzy 147br, Candice Hamilton 145c, Dedy Setyawan 38, DenPotisev 154, Diana Kovach 185, Difydave 149ac, Epitavi 149ar, 149al, Ganna Bozhko 11, Iefym Turkin 8, 27, ilbusca 20, Jobalou 50, 66, 180, KrimKate 146l, 147bl, LisaAlisa_ill 131, ma_rish 37, 48, 54, 88, 107, 111, 117, 126, 159, 161, 163, 174, Mara Fribus 145l, MaryliaDesign 79, nastya81 149cr, Natalia Churzina 70, Nikada 15, Rawpixel 41, robertsrob 19, venimo 25, 75, 151, Vladayoung 156, VladiCo 104, VvoeVale 149bl, 149cl, 149c, ZU_09 53; NASA: Bill Ingalls 69, 184; National Gallery of Art Washington/Ailsa Mellon Bruce Fund 168; NOIRLab: AURA/NSF/J. Fuentes 80, 132, T.A. Rector (University of Alaska Anchorage) and H. Schweiker (WIYN and NOIRLab/NSF/AURA) 121, 158; Shutterstock: anvinoart 95, J. Palys 147a; Unsplash: Adrian Pelletier 148, Arash 43, 157, Daniel Ziegener 46, 130, Daria Nepriakhina 28, 119, Luca Baggio 23, 35, 112, Lukas Schroeder 71, 85, Martin Adams 178, Wayne Low 96, 138, Wojciech Paczes 177; Waite-Smith deck, Pamela Colman Smith, Public domain, via Wikimedia Commons 134.

# THE AKASHIC RECORDS

Open the book of your soul
and discover your purpose

FROM THE BESTSELLING AUTHOR
THERESA CHEUNG

GODSFIELD

# CONTENTS

INTRODUCTION: *Time to Turn Your Page!* 6

PART ONE: *An Invitation to Read Your Akashic Records*

Chapter 1: The Akashic Records Origin Story 26
Chapter 2: Meet the Guardians of Your Galaxy 52
Chapter 3: Prepare for Your First Akashic Records Reading 60

PART TWO: *Discover Your Akashic Pathway*

Chapter 4: Guided Meditation 76
Chapter 5: Chakra Work 89
Chapter 6: Sacred Prayer 101
Chapter 7: Dream Reading 114
Chapter 8: Intuitive Tools 127
Chapter 9: Crystal Companions 142

PART THREE: *Akashic Wisdom Unleashed*

Chapter 10: Getting the Most Out of Your Akashic Reading 152
Chapter 11: Asking Your Guides for Help 164
Chapter 12: Answers Across Time 173

INDEX 186

SUGGESTED FURTHER READING 190

ACKNOWLEDGEMENTS 191

## INTRODUCTION

# Time to Turn Your Page!

# The Book of Your Life is open

It opened, dear hopeful reader, the moment you were drawn to this book. Indeed, this is precisely why you are holding it in your hands. It is not by chance that you are right here in this moment reflecting on these introductory words. The Book of Your Life is proudly calling your name. It is sending you an official invitation to seize this precious moment and read it.

This is it. This is your chance to answer the call for the transformation you have been seeking all your life, even if you didn't realize it at the time. All the guidance, wisdom and inspiration your soul will ever need is waiting to be discovered in the Book of Your Life, also known as your Akashic Record.

Your Akashic Record contains an energetic record of every choice you have made, are making and will make in the journey of your life. It is a genuine page-turner that is now open for you to read anytime, anywhere. You just need to understand how to access it. That's where this book comes in. Think of it as your Akashic instruction manual. It offers simple, practical tools to help you tap directly into the endless illumination that is the Book of Your Life.

And, as you are no longer a closed book, there can be no better time than right now to swiftly and gracefully accept that invitation.

Let's take a long, deep breath, keep calm and turn over your first page…

# Your cosmic compass

Interest in the Akashic Records has surged in recent years as increasing numbers of people want to know how and why things happen, and how to heal and empower themselves independently or from the inside out. The insight contained in your Akashic Record can help you do all that and infinitely more.

Rather like a cosmic compass, your Record can provide guidance at exactly the time you need it. This is because it is not just a passive memory bank recording the energetic or spiritual counterpart of your every thought, feeling, word and action – it also has a transformative influence on your daily life. Viewing it can show you how, in life, like-energy seeks like-energy. How the energy of your current thoughts, intentions, feelings and actions are always creating your present and attracting a potential future.

In the past, accessing the Akashic Records was believed to be a gift reserved for saints, scholars, mystics and psychics, but this is no longer the case. Due to changing times, more and more individuals have become attuned to the existence of their inner world, meaning they can confidently access their Records without an intermediary.

*Note: Akashic Record work is not a substitute for psychotherapy or other kinds of traditional support if you are dealing with depression, anxiety or trauma of any kind. If you are struggling with your mental health, please do also seek professional help.*

# What are the Akashic Records?

♦

The word Akashic originates from the Sanskrit word, *Akasha* (Sanskrit is the language of Hinduism). It has a range of meanings, including 'ether' – the most well-known – as well as 'empty space', 'heaven', 'source' and 'primary substance'. In the traditional Hindu system of medicine called Ayurveda, it is the fifth of five elements believed to be the building blocks of the cosmos and your individual existence: earth, fire, water, air and, last but by no means least, ether, or Akash.

Ether is said to be the most vital element because it is the one from which the other four originate. It is 'empty space' through which energy and sound travel without resistance and where everything connects. Vibration and sound are decisive, as it is thought the energetic vibrations of intentions, thoughts and words – and of actions that validate them – create your reality.

Your Akashic Record is encoded in this non-material, unseen dimension of existence, which is known as the etheric Akash plane. It is an endless energetic library – or storehouse, log or archive depending on the term you prefer – that records the energy vibration of your soul and its journey through life. Your past-life experiences and all that has led to your present identity are written in your Akashic Record, along with your potential futures, the possibilities waiting to be energized or changed by you.

Brimming with infinite knowing and all-seeing insight into your past, present and future, there you can find the answers to every question you've ever wanted to ask about yourself, life, the Universe and everyone and everything. You see, it is not just personal insight you can access in the Akashic Records, as it also contains knowledge of the entirety of the human experience and – way beyond that – of other universes and dimensions.

In summary, the Akashic Records are a vibrating information field that record the energetic vibrations of your soul and every other soul across time. They span eternity and catalogue everything, from the wisdom of the ancients to discoveries yet to come.

I'll give you a brief moment to process the above, as the concepts can be difficult to grasp, but rest assured the Akashic Records exist if you *believe* they do. You can access them any time you wish. Reading your Akashic Record is a deeply sacred experience that can radically change your life for the better. It can aid personal growth and bring you healing, deep wisdom and a sense of purpose. It can help you live your best life.

*Warning: The following theoretical explanation of the Akashic Records may initially sound rather esoteric – bordering on mystical 'mumbo jumbo' – but bear with me. Keep reading with an open mind and you'll soon discover that my intention is to demystify, to show rather than tell you that the Akashic Records are, in fact, extremely practical and can be applied to all aspects of your daily life.*

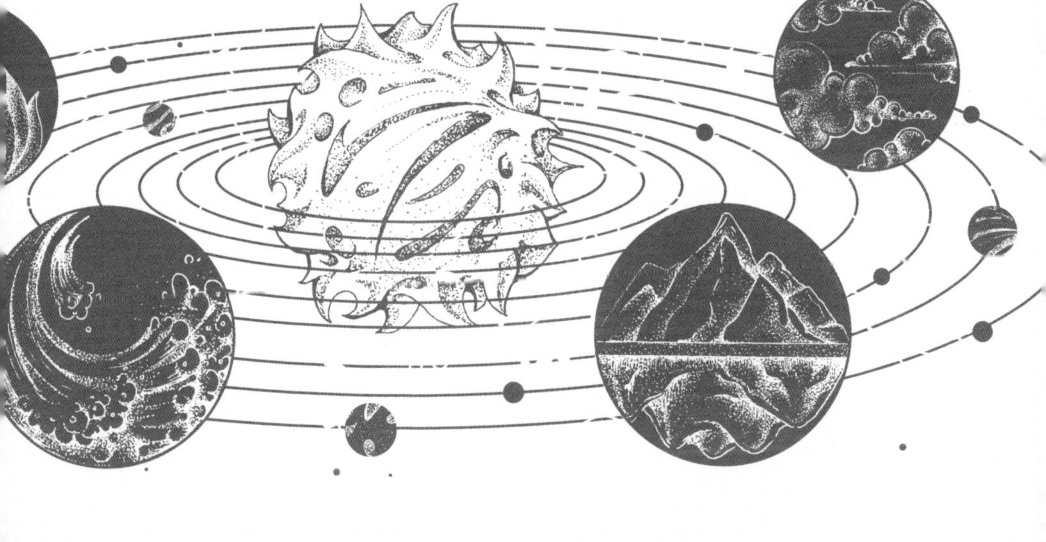

# Common misconceptions and roadblocks

The truth is, everyone can now read their book of life if they wish. Which raises the question: why isn't everybody seizing this incredible opportunity? The reason is there is still considerable uncertainty and confusion surrounding the Records. Let's purge the most common misconceptions from your awareness right now, so they can't interfere with or limit your Akashic Record work going forward.

## You can only see them when close to death or dead

This falsehood likely originates from stories of near-death experiences, or NDEs, which have become more common in recent years as increasing numbers of people are brought back from the brink of death by advances in resuscitation techniques.

The life review is a phenomenon widely reported by people who have had a near- death experience. In the few moments they are medically 'dead', or close to death, they allegedly 'see' their entire life history in an instantaneous and rapid manifestation of autobiographical memory. It is typically described by these people as 'having their life flash before their eyes'. Often that life is viewed in backwards order from present moment to birth. Others report an intense awareness of past and future lives in their life review.

It is entirely possible that the NDE 'life review' is from the Akashic Realm, but whether this is true is of no consequence. The countless numbers of people, healthy in body and mind, who access the Records on a regular basis suggests that you too can successfully access them when alive and well.

You don't have to nearly die, or experience trauma, to gain Akashic awareness, and this damaging misconception urgently needs to be laid to rest. The whole purpose of the Akashic Records is to help you see the bigger picture of your life, so you can improve it not when you are dead but while you are still alive!

### You can only access them in a trance state

Yes, you can connect to the Akashic Records in your dreams, through trance and meditation and other techniques, but you don't need to be in a semi-conscious state or take psychedelics to do this. As you will learn in this book, you can access them in simple, natural ways both when your eyes are wide shut and when they're wide open.

### They are for the gifted few

Not at all. Sure, you may well encounter people who claim they have been 'chosen' to read the Akashic Records on behalf of others. They may also claim to have special psychic powers and/or the ability to see angels or to be anointed by divinity and so on. Should you encounter such individuals, it's possible they have profound life experience, tools and advice to share. Authentic teachers and guides can be reassuring signposts on your life journey. But if at any point they place themselves on a pedestal or charge large fees for endless courses and repeat readings, or if they make you feel unworthy if you don't follow them and approach the Akashic Records their way, please steer clear.

You do not need the advice of a 'chosen one' to access the Book of Your Life. Absolutely anyone over the age of 18 can access their Akashic Record without an intermediary once they know how. Indeed, reading it your way – rather than following someone else's method – is by far the most empowering. Your direct personal experience is your greatest Akashic teacher and guide. And the best teachers are those that empower their pupils to work independently.

Every time you think of Akashic work as something reserved for the gifted few, you are damaging your self-esteem by believing that someone else is more special or more 'psychic' than you. And, as you will swiftly discover as you move through this book, whenever your self-esteem is low your chances of successfully accessing the Records dwindle.

Put simply, the greater your self-belief, the easier it is for you to read and work with the Book of Your Life. Indeed, if you have an inferiority complex and believe you're not worthy, you first need to work on your self-confidence.

## Fear of discovering negative things

Feeling anxious that you might discover negative things about yourself and your life in the Records is understandable. But repressing or denying negative impulses is the enemy of personal growth and healing. Just as there is night and day and both need each other to be whole, so there is the potential for good and evil within us all. Strength of character is having the self-awareness to acknowledge negative impulses exist within you, to understand why they are there and what they are trying to teach you, and to then choose the right path.

The Akashic Records will show you exactly what you need to acknowledge and master within yourself for personal growth. Sometimes what you discover may make you feel uneasy, but the Records were created out of unconditional love to help you face and overcome your fears so you can grow in wisdom. Working with your Akashic Record will help you become comfortable with your weaknesses, because facing and understanding them is where all personal growth starts. It will also repeatedly reinforce that just because you think or feel something does not make it so. You are not a victim of your thoughts or your feelings. The Book of Your Life will clearly reveal that you are the one in charge of your thoughts and feelings, as well as the words and actions you choose.

## It's complicated and requires special training

Reading the Akashic Records is not complicated and doesn't require intensive training. You don't need to go on a retreat or set aside two hours a day to meditate (who has the time?) or learn difficult new skills. Akashic work isn't hard and if it feels like this, then you're not doing Akashic work. The 'no pain, no gain' route to success does not apply here.

Perhaps the most beautiful thing about Akashic work is that you let go of the idea of 'struggle'. You learn to relax and simply trust the guiding wisdom in the Book of Your Life to carry you forward.

## They can give you instant solutions

Not typically. The Records can help you brainstorm and see things objectively, which can sometimes yield quick solutions. But rather than providing instant answers, their main purpose is to help you grow in self-awareness, so you understand *why* you are experiencing a certain challenge in your life and what you need to learn from it for your evolution. This understanding can then help you resolve the challenge, grow in self-knowledge and make wiser decisions going forward.

The Records teach that everything that happens to you is either a lesson or a blessing. Ironically, Akashic work will also help you relax about not knowing and not having all the answers. Indeed, mystery is the ideal condition for your evolution, because it requires you to activate the transformative and healing superpower that is your belief in yourself and your right to a happy and fulfilling life.

## They will awaken dangerous 'occult' powers

The word 'occult' has had a bad press, largely due to horror books and movies, but it simply means hidden, concealed or secret psychic powers. We all have those within us, but they only become dangerous if used negatively. And the absolute truth of Akashic Record work is that you just can't access them from a negative or fear-based mindset.

All of us are born with intuition or sixth sense – the 'psychic' ability to inexplicably sense what is unseen – but many of us lose our connection to and belief in it. Akashic work will awaken your intuition because the more you access your Records, the more your self-awareness and trust in yourself and all your untapped potential grows. In other words, the stronger your self-awareness and self-belief, the more 'psychic' you are likely to become – you will make better decisions and predict likely future outcomes. In my humble opinion, being 'psychic' is interchangeable with believing deeply in yourself. And what on Earth is wrong with that?

The Akashic Records are not dangerous. They are your best and wisest friend and guide. The fact that they have been wrongly associated with the occult is damaging, but the big clue to their integrity is that they contain *your* Akashic Record. It is your book and your life and you always have the power of choice, whatever the Book of Your Life reveals.

## They are not real

Just because you can't see something doesn't mean it is not real. You cannot see or touch love, for example, but you know it to be a real connecting and transformative force. The same goes for electricity and sound waves. And, according to physics, what you see as real or solid matter is actually over 90 per cent empty space, suggesting that your attachment to, and confidence and belief in, what you consider to be the only reality could be misplaced!

## They will show you the future

The Akashic Records are not a form of divination. Astrology and Tarot may offer better tools for that. The Records might show you *potential* futures, but their primary concern is to reveal who you are, who you believe yourself to be and who you are in the process of becoming. Everything your Record reveals is to help you examine your motives and actions and their consequences, so you can remove abundance blocks and let your soul's natural goodness attract success and happiness.

Until it manifests in real time, your Akashic future only ever exists in the realm of potential. If you don't like the future you glimpse during a reading, you have free will and the ability to change that future through the decisions you make in your present. Change your mindset and your energy will shift and attract a different future. And if you glimpse a future you want, this is a clear sign it is possible for you. When you have that level of self-belief, you are so very close to manifesting it in your daily life.

Your Akashic Record shares with you the most probable outcome based on your current direction of thinking. In other words, the Records reveal projections and possibilities. They are not prophecy. Your destiny is not fixed or written in the stars. You have free will. There is no reason why you shouldn't know your potential destiny and play your part in shaping it towards greatness.

Knowing the whole truth and only the truth about your soul is life-changing. You finally discover that only you can determine your destiny. The power of your personal choice is strong and can override any notion of fate. You are not a victim of your destiny unless you choose to be.

## You can only access your Record with a special prayer

Prayer is one tried-and-tested way to access your Akashic Record – and you will learn about sacred Akashic prayer later (see pages 101–113) – but it is not the definitive or only way. There are other effective pathways to the Book of Your Life, and this book will cover the most accessible ones in the hope you will experiment with them all until you find the path that works best for you.

## They are controlling

There is a bizarre belief that the Akashic Records can be used to manipulate people, that if someone else reads your Record they can control your mind. But this is not only inaccurate, it is also insulting. No one – and I repeat no one – can ever control your mind and/or your life without your consent.

## They are for the religious

Not so. There are associations with Hinduism in particular, but also with Buddhism, Islam and Christianity and other major world religions, but the Akashic Records do not support or contradict any one religion or culture. They belong to the cosmos. In short, you can access the Records whether you're religious or not. And they especially resonate with the increasing numbers of people who are spiritual but not religious.

## It's navel-gazing

Although Akashic work calls for self-reflection, this isn't self-indulgent because every time you become more self-aware you grow in humility and empathy towards others. You understand that everyone is just another book in the infinite Akashic library. Everyone, like you, has their own struggles and lessons to learn along the way.

In addition, the Akashic Records contain the entire history of every soul, and these Records connect each of us to one another. In the Akashic tradition of embracing opposites, you understand that we are all energetically connected. And what you think, feel and do creates energy vibrations that contribute to the collective energy of the cosmos. You are both the ocean and the drop, everything and nothing at the same time.

# About this book and how to use it

♦

We begin Part One with a brief history of the Akashic Records and their intriguing origin story. This will prepare you for your own upcoming, out-of-this-world Akashic adventure. You will get a sense of just how timeless, accessible and universal the Records are.

Then our focus will switch to the eternal timeline in your Records – how they reveal your past, present and future. We will look at reincarnation, the idea that your soul can be reborn over and over again, and why your grasp of this spiritual metaphor is key for Akashic work. Similarly, your understanding of the term 'channelling' matters, so you will find clear explanations of both reincarnation and channelling.

Along the way, you will also be introduced to the science of consciousness. Contrary to what you might think, modern science doesn't condemn or contradict Akashic work at all, rather it supports it. And after this therapeutic dose of Akashic history and science there's a timely reminder of all the self-healing benefits of accessing your Records. The reasons why you really must do it – and do it a lot.

Then you will be introduced to your Lords of the Records. These are your new spiritual friends – the invisible guardians of your own galaxy – who are waiting in the wings and eager to get to know you. They are your angels, masters, teachers and guides, lovingly dedicated to helping you fully understand the Book of Your Life. You will find out how to sense their healing powers and qualities.

Following your induction into the hall of Akashic fame, you'll discover the optimum way to prepare for your first Akashic reading. The insight here matters greatly, because to read the Book of Your Life clearly you must be in a calm, open and positive frame of mind. This isn't always easy to achieve in a material world filled with distractions, so you'll need fast-track ways to get there.

Knowing the right pathway for you to access the Akashic Records is crucial, because what will work for one person may not work for another.

That's why Part Two is dedicated to helping you find your unique Akashic pathway. You are encouraged to review the most accessible and well-reported pathways to see which one resonates most with you. There are different paths for different learners. This is your time to discover and then claim the one true path for your present stage in life; you may find as you learn and grow that another pathway speaks more clearly at a different point in your life.

Part Three explores what revelations to expect with your first Akashic readings, as well as how to frame questions for different areas of your life. You will learn how the Records often offer answers that connect your past in this life (and previous lives) to your present, to help you create a positive shift, as well as how to receive those answers in the optimum way. The Records can also give you an answer by revealing a potential future to you. The importance of a code of ethics, especially if you decide to do readings for others, will be stressed.

Throughout the book you will find practical tools punctuating the theory, along with the odd case history. You might want to read the entire book from beginning to end first, but be sure to pause and DO all the exercises in turn on a second reading and take notes as you do. It is very important that your Akashic awareness doesn't stay in your head. You need to apply what you learn in these pages to your daily life.

# In the beginning, it is your word

Over the years, I have learned that not only is everything in the Records, but there isn't just one way to access them, and at different stages of my life I have accessed them in different ways. Some of this has been done unconsciously, but increasingly in recent years I have made a conscious decision to let Akashic energy and insight flow through me, using both my favoured dreamwork pathway at night and my intuition by day.

Sometimes, during the day, simply saying the word 'Akashic' out loud or in my thoughts before an important talk or task connects me to the Records at a deep energetic level. Speaking or thinking the word reassures me that my Records are always there for me. I can receive beautiful clarity, answers and inspiration any time I want to dive deep into them.

My Akashic Record work has been and continues to be utterly life-changing. By the end of this book, you will have all the tools you need to access the Book of Your Life and change all aspects of your life for the better too. Indeed, the transformative work has already begun. Just reading the word Akashic over and over in these pages is already awakening your mind, heart and soul on multiple levels.

And when you discover what your chosen Akashic pathway is, and understand how it can help you nurture the self-awareness and inner calm you need to access your Records without fear, you have a head start. Your personal and spiritual growth will flow and feel effortless as you learn the importance of rising above, seeing the bigger picture. However tough life gets, you'll know how to transform any problems you encounter into purpose. Your life is a series of lessons and blessings, and you will discover that both are liberating.

When you achieve this sense of perspective, your transformation will accelerate at warp speed. You will become an unstoppable force. The sky will no longer be your limit.

## A NOTE ON VISUALIZATION

Some of the exercises in this book ask you to practise the art of visualization – forming mental imagery in your mind's eye when your eyes are closed. If you are one of the many people (myself included) who struggle with this, describing what you want to visualize or imagine in words to yourself (out loud or silently in your thoughts), or drawing or writing it down, are equally effective. Think of yourself as an art critic describing a work of art in a blog, or a movie critic summarizing a film. Please note that not being able to visualize when you are awake does not have any impact on your ability to recall dream images and symbols on waking.

PART ONE

# An Invitation to Read Your Akashic Records

*Akashic Wisdom Unleashed:*
*Everything that happens in the material world has its counterpart and can be observed in the spiritual world. This expansive vision is called reading your Akashic Records.*

## CHAPTER 1

# The Akashic Records Origin Story

# Understanding the Akashic Records

The general consensus is that the Akashic Records exist in an unseen spiritual dimension of consciousness. We frame this concept in the symbolic representation of a library to help our linear minds process what is interdimensional. But don't rule out the possibility of their physical manifestation.

Like the magical legends surrounding the Holy Grail or the Sword of Excalibur, it is whispered that the Records will one day be found on Earth, when enough of us have done the collective soul-level work. Suggested locations include a secret chamber buried in the Egyptian sands beneath the Great Sphinx of Giza. Although this sounds like the stuff of *Indiana Jones* or *National Treasure* movies, when you start working with the Akashic Records nothing ever feels impossible again. Indeed, your life starts to feel like an unexpected adventure.

## TAKE YOUR TIME OUT

Since time began, the Records have taken note of everyone and everything. All past, present and future possibilities are there to help you awaken and become aware of the potential for infinite light and goodness in all things. Every emotion, every thought, every deed, every choice and every step you have ever made is recorded. This is not to judge you, but to make you self-aware and conscious of the impact of your thoughts and actions. The Records simply keep a record and offer you a priceless opportunity to rise above and *observe* yourself, so you can consciously choose the path of greatest healing. From this strong Akashic objective viewpoint, you can make better life choices that elevate your soul rather than drag it down.

The three guiding principles of the Akashic Records are:

*Judge not*
*Fear not*
*Resist not*

There is no judgement, fear or resistance in the Akashic Realm, because its purpose is ultimate self-reflection and learning and evolving from what you observe. And what you 'see' will not overwhelm you, because when you do an Akashic reading, only what you can understand and need in your present moment will be revealed.

# Akashic substance

Despite growing interest in recent years, information about the substance of the Akashic Records remains fairly sparse. However, every time someone discovers them, the universal store of knowledge about them expands. Indeed, the act of faith you made in reading this book is already adding to that energetic expansion and bringing awareness of the Records ever closer to Earth. Your curiosity and willingness to open your heart and mind is more energetically significant than you realize.

The Records exist in the ether – a soul-level, non-physical realm that is the energetic life force or source energy which flows through everyone and everything, including you, nature and the Universe. But be aware that feeling the Akashic force is a mental and spiritual power rather than a physical one like moving objects with your mind (telekinesis).

As mentioned earlier (see page 10), the word *Akasha* has various meanings, but they are elusive and don't really enlighten us as to the actual 'nature' of the Akashic Records. We do know that they are infinite – an expansive 'library' of energetic information that contains records of the past, present and future of every soul that ever existed, including yours. Being in a higher dimension, the rules of logic, reason and linear time don't apply there, so what happened centuries ago is as ready to surface as what happened yesterday; what could happen in a year is as available as what happened last week.

Your Record is thought to have two components – one that is permanent and one that is always evolving. The permanent part of your Akashic Record is said to be your soul in its wholeness or enlightened, highest vibration state. The evolving part is believed to energetically record all the choices your soul makes on its learning journey towards enlightenment or the conscious realization of its fully enlightened, permanent self. In other words, you can use your Akashic Record to monitor or track the progress of the unconditional love that is your true essence, or your soul's return to love.

And the Records aren't exclusive to human souls, as they catalogue every form of life, including animals and plants, as well as the energetic vibrations of places, events, objects and even other dimensions. There truly is no beginning and no end to the knowledge contained in the Akashic Records.

# A brief history of the Akashic Records

Not surprisingly, the Records have never been completely hidden. They were familiar to many ancient cultures and societies, including the Babylonians, Assyrians, Egyptians, Persians, Chinese, Greek, Mayans, Tibetans, Indians and Phoenicians, although they may have gone by another name.

### ANCIENT EGYPT

The earliest mention of the Akashic Records probably appears in ancient Egyptian hieroglyphs, on scrolls detailing the work of revered priests who could access them and pharaohs who sought their sacred insight. The ancient Egyptians also called the Records the 'Repository of Thoth' and the goddess Seshat was known as the 'Keeper of the Library' or the 'Keeper of the Great Book of Souls'. Belief in the Records was evident in ancient Egypt even among those who could not read – dreams were decoded by ordinary Egyptians according to the wisdom gleaned from the Records.

### ANCIENT INDIA

Ancient Indian sages believed that all the natural elements were connected by the element of *Akasha* which could record every emotion, thought, deed and choice and which encompassed everything and everyone. They also believed that every soul had its own Record and that it was possible to read those Records. To this day, Indian palm leaf readers believe the lines on the leaves relate to the Akashic Records.

**MAYANS**

In Mayan culture all humans, creatures and things, including inanimate objects, had a soul that could impact the physical world (animism) and each soul was eternal and indestructible. Mayan priests and priestesses openly shared their knowledge of the Akashic Records to help ordinary people connect with them. The ancient Mayans also created a sacred prayer to help anyone access the Akashic Records from a place of inner peace.

**ISLAM**

In Islam the Akashic Records are the 'Book of Decrees'. The 'Preserved Tablet' in Islam might also be interpreted as a version of the Akashic Records – this contains all intentions and events across time. It is also believed that guardian angels are assigned to every person, to document everything about their lives.

**BUDDHISM**

The notion of Alaya consciousness in Buddhism resonates deeply with the Akashic Realm. *Alaya* is the Sanskrit term for 'without limit' or 'unending'. Alaya consciousness therefore means consciousness without limit. It is about all things in the Universe and exists within everyone and everything. It is the eternal energy, the spiritual self or soul – the spark of life, if you will – that lives forever in each individual. It is divine or source energy, too. This eternal consciousness evolves as it experiences the material. It imprints information all the time and records everything energetically in the Akashic Records.

**OTHER CULTURES AND RELIGIONS**

Indigenous Americans, Shamans and Druids all dip into the Records. In Judaism, the Old Testament mentions a 'Book of the Living', while in Christianity, the New Testament references a 'Book of Life'. It is said that this will be opened in the 'last days' and that it contains information about who will go to heaven. In the Hebrew tradition, the angel Metatron is

called the recording angel or scribe, who writes down every human deed. In the Talmud, Metatron is said to teach and guide people through heaven.

**IN THE WEST**

In Western culture, it is thought that the 16th-century physician, astrologer and seer Nostradamus – whose verses appear to predict future events, such as 9/11 – could access the Akashic Records. But the same could also be said of any visionary thinker accessing them intuitively, from Plato to Einstein to Steve Jobs and beyond.

The first strong reference to the Records in the West was towards the end of the 19th century, when Helena Petrovna Blavatsky, the Russian thought leader who founded the Theosophical Society, described a cosmic principle that contained the 'quintessence of all forms of energy – material, psychic and spiritual'. Alfred Percy Sinnett in *Esoteric Buddhism* (1883) and Henry Steel Olcott in *The Buddhist Catechism* (1881) discussed the term Akashic Record. Around the same time, Austrian philosopher and psychic Rudolf Steiner asserted that the Akashic Records were an opportunity to see beyond the material and discover a deeper counterpart spiritual reality, invisible to the human eye.

Contemporaries Alice Bailey, Charles Leadbeater and Max Heindel were also notably linked to the Akashic Records, but the leading voice at the time was the 'sleeping prophet', Edgar Cayce.

### EDGAR CAYCE

Born in 1877, Edgar Cayce was an American clairvoyant and medical intuitive. He did much to move the Akashic Records from the unconscious to the conscious realms and to popularize them as a healing tool with his 'readings'. In these readings, he relaxed into a deep, trance-like state. People would ask him medical questions and he would offer healing answers. The readings covered the past, present and future and every one was meticulously recorded by a scribe. When asked, Cayce would say that his surprisingly accurate insights came directly from the Akashic Records.

Cayce believed the Records would one day be found on Earth and that humanity was ready to create a new destiny. He only accepted voluntary donations for his readings, believing it was his responsibility to serve the world. The Records showed him a potential future where he would fall seriously ill if he didn't reduce the number of readings he gave, but he did not slow down because so many people were asking for his help. A year later he died.

The documented records of Cayce's readings are available in book form and online. They showcase his belief in the individual and the expansive nature of the Records. They show that the Records exist within and all around us, how we can access and learn from them, and how our actions in mind, body and soul are constantly imprinting information.

## MORPHIC RESONANCE

Everyone has their own energetic record. And it's not just humans – animals, plants, elements, names, objects and places also have vibrational records. Even just thinking about a person, place or thing sends them energy. Just as electromagnetic fields can influence the material they surround, so your personal energetic field doesn't just influence your life, but also the lives of others. This is known as morphic resonance.

According to scientist Rupert Sheldrake, who coined the term morphic resonance in the 1980s in his book *A New Science of Life*, morphogenic fields contain the energy of both individuals and groups, and these energetic fields create a collective consciousness that influences all those who come into contact with the group. Over time, this morphic resonance creates behavioural changes that take on a life of their own, and in some cases move the human race in a different energetic direction.

This concept underlines the fact that you do not live in isolation. What you think, feel and do impacts not just your life but the lives of others in energetic ways you may not fully understand. You have the power not just to clear your own unloving energy, but to direct loving energy towards others, too. Every time you feed yourself and others healing energies, these expand and shift both your life and the life of others – and potentially the world – in a loving direction.

# Everchanging times

Today anyone can connect directly to their Akashic Record without reverting to religion or dogma. If you truly wish to access it, you can. And you don't have to turn to people entering a trance state or altered states of consciousness like Edgar Cayce. Due to changing times creating a related energetic shift, you can be fully conscious and wide awake while connecting to the Records.

You can access the Records to connect with your undiscovered creative potential, but the most profound connection is with your own higher consciousness, or soul. Your soul helps you see that your life is constantly offering you limitless opportunities to learn, change and evolve into higher awareness. And every time you shift your awareness from the material world and see beyond the physical to your true inner power, you dramatically change your life.

This is the awesome power of the Akashic Records. Understanding the influence of your past on your present identity offers you an opportunity to shape your future. You realize that the power is within you to overcome challenges, heal and find meaning. All you need to do to access this wonderful source material is *believe* in it and then *prepare* yourself to receive the information. And, as you will see on pages 60–73, where I share the simple things you can do every day to become more receptive to the Akashic Records, preparing yourself to access and receive information is not difficult. It's a natural process of unfolding.

In summary, over time the history of the Akashic Records has moved from exclusive to inclusive and from unconscious to conscious. They are open all the time for everyone. What a wonderful time it is to be alive!

# The science of consciousness

*The Turning Point* is a pioneering book by Austrian-born American physicist Fritjof Capra, published in 1982. In it, he proposed the existence of a 'shared consciousness' in everyone and everything, but which also takes into account individual consciousness. Other terms with the same meaning include 'cosmic consciousness' or 'the universal mind'. Capra's proposal led the way for other visionary scientists to also posit that consciousness – the life force within everyone and everything – is a vibrating field of vibrant energetic information forever changing and expanding in response to information from and observation of the material world. It can also vibrate in resonance with others.

Quantum physics is now successfully proving that observation, information and communication can create mysterious energetic connections. And this, in essence, encapsulates the timeless, all-encompassing, shared but individual nature of the Akashic Records and their ability to forever expand with every personal and shared contribution to them.

Indeed, the energy and consciousness principles of quantum physics mirror the Akashic Realm. The Heisenberg uncertainty principle – which states that the Universe is not static but in a state of constant flux or flow and that change is always happening – quantifies the ever-present potential for change. All future outcomes exist as energetic potential and even the smallest of changes can create a course correction.

We should also note the many-worlds interpretation of quantum mechanics here, which suggests that there are parallel universes, and for every action taken, there are an infinite number of universes that coexist at the same time in which we do not take that action. (If you've watched movies like *Sliding Doors, Dr Strange in the Multiverse of Madness* or *Everything, Everywhere, All At Once,* you'll find this idea of parallel universes explored in entertaining ways.)

Unless you are a physicist, all this may sound rather daunting, but put simply, the ultimate goal of Akashic work is to help you understand the source of your own inner compass to direct your life. The Records are within you and you are within the Records, and accessing the energetic imprint recorded there to find out where you have been, where you are now and where you are likely going is a revelation.

In quantum physics and in life, like-energy attracts like-energy. Understanding your current energetic history, and what it is attracting into your life, through an Akashic reading offers you a priceless opportunity. Through a reading, you can clear away unhealthy energy from your personal Record and in the process heal your life by replacing what does not serve you with healthy energy instead. And making that energy switch is simple. It is a matter of consciously choosing loving and positive thoughts, feelings and actions, whatever life throws at you.

And remember, given consciousness is shared, every time you heal and evolve from the inside out, it isn't just about you any more. It also helps heal others energetically and perhaps even the cosmos, too.

# You'll be back

♦

The Akashic Records ask you to believe in or be open-minded about reincarnation, the notion that your soul has had many lives – that when you die your soul or consciousness is reborn and lives another lifetime on Earth. You may be familiar with this concept from the book and movie *Cloud Atlas*. The Akashic Records can reveal your past lifetimes because sometimes past-life trauma is encoded in your Records and reactivated in your current lifetime when you experience a situation or relationship that reminds you of a past life. It will continue to do that until you recognize the repeating pattern and change your mindset.

Of course, the theory of reincarnation has yet to be proved, but the research is compelling – for example, the 1957-onwards studies conducted by Dr Ian Stevenson and his team at the University of Virginia of thousands of young children who reported past-life memories and dreams which proved to be remarkably accurate. It is well worth checking out those studies.

You may also want to take a moment to consider the scientific law of conservation of energy. This doesn't refer to saving energy, but to energy never being created or destroyed. When energy is used it does not disappear or 'die'. Instead, it changes from one form of energy to another. So, the theory that when you die the energy of your consciousness can transform and potentially live on in the afterlife and/or be reborn in another body doesn't sound so far-fetched, does it?

And in many ways reincarnation does offer a satisfying explanation for experiences that we struggle to explain rationally. For instance, that feeling of familiarity with someone you have only just met, or when visiting a place and feeling as if you've been there before. The term we use for that is déjà vu, or déja rêvè if you were there before in a dream. Perhaps you have met that person or been there before in a dream or another lifetime?

If you struggle to embrace the idea of reincarnation, simply opening your mind to it as another infinite possibility yet to be proven is a great starting point, as is approaching it as a spiritual metaphor for being reborn in every present moment. Sometimes, even reflecting on your childhood,

*Note: A timely reminder that Akashic Record work is not a substitute for psychotherapy or other kinds of traditional support if you are dealing*

or a decade ago, can feel like a foreign country, another lifetime and place where things felt and were done differently.

When you access your Akashic Records you encounter your 'eternal timeline'. This is your past, present and future, which may be happening all at once, a linear-time-defying notion supported by Einstein. This expansive sense of yourself, or your 'long body' stretched across time according to Shamanic culture, gives you an out-of-this-world opportunity to stop wasting energy on trying to control what is transient and happening outside you, and to focus instead on what is always happening within you.

# Karma

Karma goes hand in hand with reincarnation. Your soul may need a lot of lifetimes on its journey to a higher state of being or to recognizing its true nature. Buddha was said to have had a thousand lives before he reached enlightenment. In Sanskrit the word *karma* means deed or action, while in Hinduism and Buddhism *karma* is the relationship between a person's mental or physical actions and the energetic consequences following that action. In short, the good you do will come back to you, as will the bad.

Karma is often defined as the law of cause and effect, but it is really about the accumulated vibrational or energetic impact of all the choices you make through your thoughts, intentions, feelings, words and actions. These create patterns that can attract experiences which either challenge or bring happiness.

Karma is your energetic history that directs your life in the present and the future. Understanding the impact of accumulated karma gives you the incentive to change your present energetic vibration. Let go of what no longer serves you, discover untapped potential and redirect your energy to change your life and attract the future you want.

Past-life karma can be the reason for negative patterns or relationships. Your past self may have done something damaging that imprinted itself on your energetic Record where it continues to exert a negative influence over your present. The good news is that when you discover the cause through an Akashic reading, you become aware and can fix matters. You can find out what you need to make right to ease your karmic burden.

While karma refers to accountability, reincarnation embodies opportunity. Your soul gets a chance to repay its karmic debt. It will continue to be reborn until it reaches enlightenment.

Karma is, of course, a philosophy familiar in Hinduism and Buddhism. You either believe in it or you don't. But you have everything to gain by being open-minded. The more of us who believe that what we put out is what will be reflected back at some point in our life, the less cruelty and suffering there will be in the world.

## REWRITE YOUR AKASHIC HISTORY

When you access your Akashic Records with a question about a specific aspect of your life, and they reveal negative scenes from the past to help you understand how they've led to your present, you can do something radical. You can step back in time and rewrite that past.

Simply imagine or write down a better outcome, so you emerge empowered rather than weakened. For example, if you recently had an argument and lost your temper, you can revisit the argument in your mind and imagine that you didn't lose your temper. Doing this will help you remove and heal any energy blockages in your past Akashic Records, so you can start to rescript them and liberate your present from their depleting influence.

# Back to your future

Your Akashic Record may initially reveal your present rather than your past, revealing your current behaviour and thought patterns, so you can better understand the positive or negative energy they are imprinting on your Records and the implications of the current choices you are making. You can't rewrite your present as it is in flux, but moving forward you can resolve to change your behaviour and mindset to raise your vibration and improve your life.

One thing is certain: if you are currently ruled by a negative mindset, this will be creating karma for your future. Viewing your present Records can offer you clarity on why this is happening and – more often than not – you'll find that it is connected to feelings of not being worthy. Chances are, you are focusing the energy of your thoughts and feelings on what you don't want to manifest, not on what you do. Not surprisingly, the energy of what you don't want is therefore more likely to occur in the future.

Acknowledging that everything you think, feel and do doesn't only impact your present but also your future is a huge incentive to invest in a healthy dose of positive thinking and living, whatever life throws at you. And if you get to view a potential future that fills you with fear, remember the Records are there to inform, guide and heal you. They are showing you how your soul's current energy is creating your future Records, but those future Records are ever-changing. The future you see is only a possibility and it is up to you to act on it or not. For example, Edgar Cayce was shown a future in which he had health problems due to the stress of doing too many Akashic Readings for others (see page 34). If he had heeded that warning and slowed down, he may not have died a year later.

Whenever you make changes in your present, your future Akashic Records will change too. You may start to see happier outcomes, but if this doesn't happen immediately, just give yourself time. Change does not happen overnight and can sometimes take a while to imprint itself on your Records. You can help positive change along by consciously visualizing or writing down a future where you 'see' yourself thriving. And the great thing about that future is you can revisit it at any time and add more and more details, to ensure it is the positive future you deserve. Every time you do this, you strengthen its energy vibration and permanent presence in your future Records.

Here is another empowering thought: your present self is at some point going to become the past for your future self to view. Now you understand the energetic consequences of your present thoughts and actions on your future self, you have every reason to make a *conscious* decision to choose honesty, positivity, compassion, joy and unconditional love for yourself and others in this present moment. Plus, studies show that when people believe they are being observed their performance improves. It is called the Observer Effect. Well, you are being observed all the time by your future self, so it's always the right time to impress yourself!

## THE POWER OF CHOOSING LOVE

Research published in the *Consciousness and Cognition* journal shows that viewing scenes as if they are happening outside your body activates key pathways in your brain that ignite creativity, self-belief and hope. When people visualize past or future versions of themselves, they do so with less judgement than when they view themselves in the present.

Taking this observational stance is what happens naturally whenever you access your Akashic Records. Add to this research published in the *Journal of Anomalous Experience and Cognition,* which suggests unconditional love for yourself and others enhances the accuracy of precognition (sensing the future), and you have yourself the winning manifesting combination required to access your Akashic Records. Self-awareness, self-love and self-belief.

# No less than the trees and stars

The elements that formed the stars billions of years ago also formed your DNA. We are all stardust in that sense and every one of the cells in your body carries a memory, records of you and your ancestral roots. Your Akashic Records also imprint all your emotions, beliefs and actions along the way. Patterns are formed and the more emotional the experience, the more influential your Record becomes until you take action to change it. That is why Akashic Record work is so refreshing, because once you can identify a pattern that isn't working you can change it. You can rewrite your destiny into one that is empowering and rich in terms of your eternal worth. You can heal ancestral trauma, change your present and empower your future self.

Choosing compassion, forgiveness, wisdom and love instead of negativity is self-mastery, and it is also how you evolve, step off the karmic wheel and ascend into higher and higher levels of consciousness, which is your true nature. A sign you are heading in the right direction is that you think less of yourself as body with a soul and more of yourself as a soul with a body.

# Follow the feeling

Along with the tried-and-tested metaphor of a master library with a book for everything, you can also think of the Akashic Records as a vast energetic data system. Rather like a giant energetic invisible computer that records and stores the data of all that has happened and is happening, while constantly calculating projections about what may come to pass. And not just on Earth but in the galaxy and other dimensions as well.

Later you will learn how to prepare for and access the Akashic Records – turning that computer on and finding the relevant pages in the Book of Your Life (see page 78). But an important part of accessing the Records is connected to your intuition or sixth sense, or how you sense or perceive beyond your five physical senses of sight, hearing, smell, touch and taste.

Intuition is knowing something without finding any rational reason for why you should. For example, you might sense without any reason that someone you haven't heard from in years is going to text you and within a few moments they do! It is listening to your gut instinct and feelings and what insights come to you. It is not interpreting information or making calculated guesses, but about being open to receiving spontaneous insight that just bursts through seemingly out of nowhere.

Sometimes that insight may speak to you through your body's wisdom and the spiritual energy centres in your body known as chakras (see pages 89–100 for more on chakras and using chakra energy work to access the Akashic Records).

# Channelling

To successfully access the Records, you need to suspend disbelief and raise your energy to match a higher dimension of knowledge. Belief that the Records exist is key, as is a belief that you're worthy enough to access them. In essence, you need to expand your mind and open your heart, so you can tune into the energetic frequency of the information you seek. You need to leave three-dimensional reality behind and step (metaphorically speaking) into the ether.

The Records are a state of mind rather than a place, an experience rather than a concept. Meditation is one way to consciously raise your vibration, but any time you are listening to your intuition, you are unconsciously accessing the Akashic Record. That is why understanding how your intuition speaks to you is a key part of working with the Records, because you can't think yourself into them. Instead, you need to relax and allow intuitive information to pour into your heart. When that happens, the term commonly used is channelling.

There's plenty of scientific research to back up the reality of channelling. Perhaps channelling happens because we are all energetically interconnected and your behaviours and choices – both unconscious and conscious – co-create the reality of what you experience.

Everyone has the ability to channel in some way. However, the way you channel information from the Akashic Records will differ from someone else's. There are many ways to channel, ranging from listening to your gut instinct to trance channelling. The guided meditation section of this book (see pages 76–88) shares some common channelling pathways to experiment with when you want to access the Records.

# Benefits of accessing the Akashic Records

I'm aware that this chapter has been rather concept-heavy, so to get you out of your head and back into your life here's a run-down of 12 life-changing benefits of Akashic work (see overleaf). But there are many more, and I hope in time you can add your long list of healing reasons why to this overview.

### Takeaway time

Akashic Record work can open you up to a whole new world of unlimited joy and possibilities. You have read this far, so I can only assume you are fully invested and have made the decision to search for guidance in the Akashic Realm. I am beyond excited for you. I have no idea what lies ahead for you, as the Akashic adventure is always an unexpected one filled with surprises, but of one thing I am certain: your life will never be the same again.

If you take anything away from the theory so far, let it be that you are more than your body and your mind. Your consciousness can transcend your body and your mind as well as logic, reason, linear time and space itself. This 'rising above' to meet and greet your spiritual self happens every time you access your Akashic Records.

Cling tight to that transcendent feeling as the next chapter will (metaphorically speaking) give you wings.

1. Knowing how to access your Records offers you the highest form of guidance on tap, whenever you need it.
2. You get to see the bigger picture of your life and are less likely to become caught up in energy-draining human dramas.
3. You become more self-aware, which is the beginning of all wisdom. This self-awareness brings you more independence, assertiveness and resilience.
4. You understand that your energy – what you believe to be true about yourself – is the energy you tend to attract and if you want to change your life for the better, you need to start with your own mindset. (Akashic Record work is a neglected manifesting tool.)
5. Learning about past lives can help you discover more about yourself and heal negative patterns.
6. Accessing the Records can improve your relationships, because you can identify what might be causing blocks. The Records also help you recognize issues that are preventing you from attracting success and happiness in all other aspects of your life.
7. Learning about potential futures can help you course-correct and point you in the right direction.
8. You can use the Records to help you make decisions and find answers to all your questions, including those you have about other people, situations and any future outcome, including world events.
9. You can discover untapped creative potential and inner strength within yourself that you didn't know existed.
10. You understand how to view problems as opportunities for learning and this constant process of soul evolution gives your life deep purpose and meaning.
11. Trusting in something bigger than yourself – that is the source of all knowledge – is both comforting and confidence boosting, offering you a healthy dose of self-belief and a sense of meaning and purpose that may have been missing before.
12. The Records offer you a safe place, a sanctuary, where time and material concerns melt away and you can find inner peace. This is deep, soul-level healing.

## CHAPTER 2

# Meet the Guardians of Your Galaxy

# Is this the real thing?

♦

Before we dive in much further, I must introduce you to your Akashic spiritual support team. It is important that you can immediately recognize and sense their supportive energy potential whenever you access your Records.

Yes, in this chapter we will be talking about angels and other spiritual beings of light that can travel to the Akashic Realm to guide and assist you. You have every right to remain sceptical. Belief in spirit guides is a deeply personal thing. Some people believe in them completely and think they can manifest on rare occasions in the material world; others see them as more of a spiritual metaphor. And some don't believe in them at all. No belief is right or wrong.

I believe in angels – always have, always will – but not in the traditional wings-and-halo sense. I prefer to think of them as beautiful symbols of the eternal forces of goodness, love and light in the cosmos. I also regard them

as the purest and highest energetic forces within me and everyone and everything. But whether you believe in angels as spiritual beings that visit the Akashic ether, or as aspects of yourself and the potential for goodness within you waiting to be activated, is actually immaterial. What matters is not so much a belief in their reality but your belief in what they *represent*, which is the energy of goodness and unconditional love within and all around you.

So, without further ado, let me introduce you to the guardians of your own Akashic galaxy. As you meet each in turn, visualize what they might look like and/or consider how they may make you feel should they cross your path in an Akashic reading. Don't be surprised if they all feel vaguely familiar. This is because on a deep soul level you have met them before and already know them well.

Every time you have ever felt unconditional love, joy, empathy and compassion, or had a blissful eureka moment of illumination, they have been right there celebrating with you. You just didn't know their names. Let's correct that now, so the next time they fly into your heart you can greet them confidently by name. You'll also find out about their true spiritual nature and the important roles they wish to play in your life.

*Note: Be aware that there is an optimum way to ask your spiritual guidance team questions, and you will learn how to do* *that on pages 155–158.*

# The Lords of the Records

Let's start right at the top or highest point with the Lords of the Records. They are the gatekeepers and they are the protectors of the Akashic Records. They have the authority to let people read their Records or to refuse entry to someone who is not ready to enter. They are pure beings of light, and their purpose is to help people reach their highest potential.

The Lords of the Records also decide what information to reveal to you. They will withhold information if it is not relevant or you're not ready to receive it. They are always observing and watching over you, but as everyone's Records are protected by the Lords, they are not specific to you. They 'translate' the Akashic Records into language you can understand. They take your questions to the Records and then return to you with an answer that will make sense to you.

They won't reveal themselves, but will pass on the information they want you to know through other spiritual guides: the Masters, Teachers and Departed Loved Ones (see page 56). Whenever you feel a transcendent sense of deep interconnection with everyone and everything and empathy for the collective, you are tuning into the blissful vibration of the Lords of the Records.

# Masters, Teachers and Departed Loved Ones

The Masters are beings of light who protect the learning and growth of your soul, wanting you to evolve to your highest potential. They have the power to select and call for the help of Teachers and Departed Loved Ones on your behalf. Whenever you have a eureka moment in your Akashic work, chances are the Masters are the source.

Some commonly reported Ascended Masters – meaning those spiritually enlightened beings who once lived on Earth, such as Christ, Krishna, Mohammed and Buddha – are strongly associated with the spiritual truths of the religions they founded. Others, such as the ancient philosopher Aristotle, the wizard Merlin of Arthurian legend and Saint Teresa of Ávila, a 16th-century Spanish nun and mystic, are linked to universal wisdom, healing, discipline and self-mastery.

The Teachers may have had human lives once, but in their spirit form they chose to help human beings connect to their souls. Unlike the Lords and Masters who are always there, the Teachers are only with you until you learn a specific lesson. Then they will fly away to their next mission and another Teacher will be assigned to you by the Masters for your next lesson. The Teachers could be people you once knew or admired from afar, but they prefer you not to know who they are as they believe knowing their identity is not needed for your soul's growth. Whenever you feel excited or curious to know or do more, make a positive decision, or perform or notice or feel inspired by an act of kindness in your daily life, you are tuning into the inspiration of your Akashic Teachers.

Your Departed Loved Ones are the spirits of people who were connected to you in some way before they died. They might be deceased parents, partners or friends, but they only reveal their identity if they feel it will be helpful for you. Even if they only knew you for a brief time on Earth, you should understand that they chose to be a guardian of your soul. Your Departed Loved Ones are there whenever you feel that you're not alone. You can't explain how, but your heart senses it has been hugged.

# Your A-Team

Angels are beings of love and pure light that have never incarnated on Earth. They have a strong energetic affinity with the Akashic Realm because they carry the purest vibrations of courage, peace and unconditional love. You can create close bonds with your angels by asking them questions or calling for their help every day. They will always be there and willing to offer you their love and guidance. You just need to ask them.

There is no limit to the number of guides in spirit you could also call on for help – from Departed Loved Ones to animal guides to famous people, you may even have met them before. For example, if you need inspiration you can call on the spirit of Einstein, Marie Curie, Thomas Edison or Elvis. See pages 169–170 for advice on how to call on your angels, Ascended Masters or anyone in spirit to assist your Akashic reading, even the spirit of your beloved pet dog.

## Your higher self

Perhaps the most transformative energy you can call on for assistance in an Akashic reading is your higher self. This doesn't mean higher in that it is superior, but rather a dimension of your existence that is vibrating at a higher energy than your physical self. It has the clearest and most powerful connection to everything in the Akashic Realm and the direction in which your soul needs to move. It already knows who you are and what you need and has all the answers you're seeking.

Doubt and fear may block your connection to your higher self, so turn to page 67 for a meditation to help you silence these feelings. Use this meditation to call on your higher self to raise your vibrations, so you can calmly and lovingly access the Akashic Realm.

# How will you know?

♦

In an Akashic reading you will know when a guardian from the Akashic galaxy is present, because you will feel a profound inner shift. And that heightened awareness will almost always be associated with feelings of deep certainty, comfort, peace and calm. Fear will disappear. Your thoughts and energy will elevate.

You may also feel a slight tingling sensation at the top of your head or just above it, or a fluttering in your stomach or heart. On rare occasions you may see glimpses of bright light or colours gently flashing in the corners of your eyes, or behind your eyelids if they're closed. There may even be a subtle sweet scent of flowers or the sensation of someone staring at you. But whether or not your physical senses are activated, the most significant sign is that for reasons you can't explain, you won't feel alone in your Akashic reading any more.

And if you feel a wave of unconditional love wash over you, or experience a burst of spontaneous euphoric joy during the reading, rest assured your Akashic guides are fully present with you. If in any doubt, ask your heart: it always knows – and often long before you do – when it has been touched by the presence of an angel.

# No place like home

The next chapter will help you prepare for your first Akashic reading and every reading after that. Don't be tempted to skip it. Before anything in your Akashic reading (as in life) preparation is the key to success.

If you have ever watched the iconic movie *The Wizard of Oz*, starring Judy Garland as Dorothy, you could regard the next chapter in this book as the final but crucial black-and-white scene-setting before you immerse yourself in a new world of glorious Technicolor, which is when the real adventure begins.

This isn't to suggest that the Akashic Records are simply a vivid dream like the land of Oz, but they certainly share the same sense of infinite possibility, magic and wonder. And, just as Dorothy discovers that the answers she's been seeking and the power she needed to return home had been hers all along, so your Akashic readings will help you find your own answers and inner truth. Time and time again, they will take you back home to your soul and remind you that the power lies within you – always has and always will.

## CHAPTER 3

# Prepare for Your First Akashic Records Reading

# Your Akashic preparation template

✦

In the timeless words of visionary inventor and scientist Alexander Graham Bell: 'Before anything else, preparation is key to success.' And nowhere is this more true than when doing your first Akashic reading and further readings after that. Akashic Record work requires ongoing spiritual discipline. The following rules are non-negotiable: ignore them and you won't be able to access, let alone read, your Records.

### START FORMING DAILY HABITS

Cultivate a receptive and open mind in your everyday life. This will make the Records more accessible. Read and reread this book and lose yourself in the illustrations until the information contained in these pages enters your heart, mind and soul and belief in your Akashic Records sinks deeper and deeper into your heart.

### PRACTISE MEDITATION

Meditate for a couple of minutes each day, as study after study show that regular meditation benefits both body and mind. It can also increase your intuition, with research suggesting that some people have a psychic experience following a few weeks of daily meditation after never having had one before. In fact, brain scans indicate that meditation activates the part of the brain linked to creativity and intuition. This is the part of your brain that will help you read your Records.

If you don't wish to meditate, a few moments of deep breathing every hour or so can help clear your mind and bring a sense of inner balance. And as much as possible remind yourself during the day that you're not your thoughts or your feelings – you are in charge of these. You don't have to judge or criticize yourself, worry or become anxious. Instead, you can always decide to observe yourself and rise above.

#### FIND YOUR CALM

If you are stressed or unsettled, perform the *Wisdom of the Heart Meditation* on page 67 until you feel peaceful. Or find another way to relax, such as listening to music, taking a warm bath, drinking a cup of tea or giving yourself a hand massage with rose- or lavender-scented hand cream.

#### GET A JOURNAL

Keep a journal and a pen close by, so when you've finished a reading you can immediately record any information that comes through.

#### WORK ON THAT SELF-BELIEF

Remind yourself constantly that you're worthy and that the Akashic Records are within your reach. They are not for the gifted few. They're for the unique miracle of DNA that is you. Indeed, there is only one you and that is your superpower.

#### AVOID ALCOHOL

This must be avoided for at least 24 hours before a reading. Drinking alcohol limits your ability to control your emotions and think rationally. And it contradicts the aim of your reading, which is to help you see the truth of your life clearly. Plus, the Lords of the Records might interpret drinking alcohol as a sign of disrespect to them, the Records and yourself. The same applies to any kind of recreational drug. Prescription drugs are permitted, however, as they won't interfere with your ability to access and read your Records.

#### FIND A SAFE ENVIRONMENT

You need to find a quiet place where you won't be disturbed to consult the Records. Your Akashic work is private and between you and you alone. If you live in a busy household, this may mean getting up before everyone else or choosing to retire somewhere where you can be alone. You need to switch from focusing on what is going on around you to what is going on within you, and the best way to do that is to be alone, away from other people and distractions.

#### SWITCH OFF YOUR TECH

It goes without saying that you will need to silence all your phones and other devices when doing Akashic Record work. You need silence and peace and to be liberated from the constant demands of technology.

#### GET COMFORTABLE

It may sounds obvious but make sure you have visited the bathroom first, as you don't want any physical distractions. It's also important that you're not hungry or thirsty. Having said that, avoid doing a reading right after a meal as this may make you feel too sleepy. When you are in your quiet place, sit down and make yourself as comfortable as possible. If you prefer to lie down, that can work too, but ensure you remain alert and are not in danger of falling asleep.

#### GET A GOOD NIGHT'S SLEEP

Before a reading make sure you're well rested and not sleep-deprived. The energy of the Records is incredibly fast and the more work you can do beforehand to raise your energy vibration and feel physically and mentally refreshed, the better.

#### USE YOUR LEGAL NAME

You will need to use your legal name to access your Akashic Records. This is not your nickname and may not necessarily be your birth name. It is the current name on your passport, tax return, driver's licence and other legal documentation. When a name becomes legal it creates a vibrational identity that is recorded in your Records. Should you ever feel that your name does not resonate with you, consider changing it legally before you access your Records.

#### KNOW YOUR TIME LIMITS

Decide how much time you plan to spend in your Records ahead of each reading and then stick to that. This is all about setting clear intentions and boundaries, which is important not just for your Akashic work but also for your everyday life. You may want to set a timer, so you know when the allotted time is up and you need to close the reading. Make sure the timer is a gentle one and not a harsh-sounding or jarring sound.

#### START SMALL

You may only want to spend five or ten minutes on your first reading, as you need to get used to the Akashic high-energy vibration. Doing too much too soon may be overwhelming or make you feel spaced out. Then when you become acclimatized, you could add another five minutes, so you spend 10 or 15 minutes in the Records. You can keeping adding another five minutes to the time, but don't fall into the trap of thinking quantity is quality. Fifteen clear minutes is better than 45 murky ones. In short, go slowly and steadily at your own pace.

### START PLANNING

As well as planning in advance how much time you'll spend in your Records, plan how often you will do a reading and at what time of day. There is no right or wrong here. You can do a reading every day or every week or every month. Just decide how often works for you, then block out time in your schedule and stick to it. I prefer early evening, but you may choose early morning or a time when you feel most energized. Experiment until you find the time of day that works best for you.

### PREPARE FOR THE SENSATIONS

You may feel a gentle pressure at the crown of your head, as if information is flowing through you, or a tingling sensation in the middle of your forehead or in your heart or your stomach – your second brain. Or you may experience a deep sense of knowing or even see images of your life play out behind your eyes. Or you may experience something entirely different.

### PAY ATTENTION

Give your Akashic Record reading your full attention whenever it is in progress. Keep your eyes, mind and heart solely focused on your Records.

### GROUND YOURSELF AND PRACTISE GRATITUDE

When your planned time in the Records is up, always close the reading with gratitude and ground yourself. This is extremely important because you have shifted to the Akashic state of consciousness, and the energy vibration is higher there than in everyday life. You need to return to your daily life. If you don't, you may feel disorientated and a little spaced out, not to mention highly sensitive. It is very simple to ground yourself. Just do something that reconnects you to your body and reminds you that you're a human being. For example, drink a glass of water, eat a piece of fruit, go for a short walk, do some stretching, and so on.

# The power of your heart

♦

An important part of preparing for a reading is to become more conscious of your beating heart and to tune into your heart wisdom as often as possible. The thoughts that swirl around in our heads tend to dominate our everyday lives. This is not necessarily a bad thing if you need to plan and organize, as long as you don't become trapped in the cycle of judgement, worry and criticism that can drown out the voice of your intuition – which is the voice of your heart. The *Wisdom of the Heart Meditation* opposite can help you find that essential harmony between your logic and intuition, your thoughts and feelings.

According to the HeartMath Institute, when your heart beats calmly and steadily you're in a state of heart coherence, and this is the optimum state, not just for your physical well-being but also for your intuition to surface and help you access your Akashic Records.

Stress, fear and self-doubt are proven intuition roadblocks. To counteract them, I suggest you practise the meditation every day, ideally a few minutes before a reading. It will help silence your interfering mind, so you're open and receptive to what an Akashic reading can reveal. If you are new to meditation, it is the perfect starting point and if you repeat it daily you'll find that you become less and less distracted by your thoughts. Quieting your mind and tuning into the power of your heart will happen swiftly and naturally whenever you feel overwhelmed.

## Wisdom of the heart meditation

**STEP 1** Find somewhere quiet where you can sit comfortably and safely relax. Set a timer for three to five minutes, depending on your schedule.

**STEP 2** Tense your entire body and then relax your neck, shoulders and face. Many of us frown constantly without even realizing it. (If you have more time, do a progressive body relaxation by tensing each part of your body in turn.)

**STEP 3** Switch your attention to your breath. Take deeper than normal breaths in and out from your stomach rather than your chest.

**STEP 4** Notice how your thoughts make you feel and what direction they are heading, but don't interact with them in any way. Let them flow by.

**STEP 5** Close your eyes and continue to breathe deeply and, with each out breath, visualize or tell yourself that your thoughts are drifting away.

**STEP 6** When you feel relaxed enough and your thoughts no longer control you, shift your attention from your breath to your heart. Notice how it is beating and flow with that rhythm.

**STEP 7** Feel unconditional love right in the centre of your heart and let that love fill you and your heart. Notice how natural, familiar and peaceful a heart filled with love feels. Allow the love from your heart to flow into every part of your body. Then imagine your heart is the organ you breathe with. You are inhaling and exhaling through your heart.

**STEP 8** Open your eyes and know that your heart is an eternal source of peace and inspiration, and you can connect to it at any time.

The Records are imprinted with the memory and power of your eternal heart, or your soul and all the higher energy vibrations of wisdom, courage, creativity, compassion, integrity and love to which you aspire. And whenever your heart is calm and you feel at peace, you can access the Records. The Book of Your Life opens and is waiting to be read through the wisdom of your own heart. In other words, through your intuition.

# Empower your inner psychic

Knowing how your intuition speaks to you during an Akashic reading is vital, because otherwise you may not notice it. Most of us think that psychic information comes through external visions and voices, but that is rarely the case.

Intuition speaks to you from the inside out. And the subtleness of this inner wisdom during a reading is its power. It forces you to concentrate fully and reflect deeply on the meaning beneath the surface, the material, or in other words what ego, logic and reason have ignored but which is important for your personal and spiritual growth.

You concentrate when you want to listen carefully and narrow your eyes when you wish to focus. You already have a wonderful ability to focus with your physical senses of hearing, smelling, seeing, tasting and touching and you can do the same with your intuition. You can learn to consciously focus your attention on the way it is trying to talk to you. When you receive information in an Akashic reading, pay close attention to *how* it comes through. Is it visual? Is it through sound? Is it through sensation? Is it through knowing?

There is considerable crossover, but you may find that one way of connecting to your intuition feels more natural than another. Knowing this can be very helpful, because focusing on just a single intuitive technique to access the Records – one that requires you, for example, to visualize when you're more receptive to sounds and voices – is going to block your progress.

## KNOW YOUR CLAIRS!

Your intuition can speak in many ways, but for the purpose of clarity here are the four main routes:

*Clairvoyance or clear seeing* You may notice energy colours and patterns and visions with your eyes open, but clear seeing typically manifests when your eyes are closed. You see images behind your eyes and typically experience vivid dream recall. You are a seer. In everyday life, visualization and daydreaming may come naturally to you.

*Clairaudience or clear hearing* You tune into a world of inner sound. You can't get a word, sound, quote, song or voice out of your head. You are an oracle. Listening to music you love gives you goose bumps and overhearing conversations or sounds can sometimes trigger meaningful coincidences.

*Claircognizance or clear knowing* This is inner resolve. You don't know why, but you just know the answer or what you need to do or what is going to happen next or what someone else will say or do. You are a knower. In everyday life, you can often sense the future before it happens.

*Clairsentience or clear sensing* This is when your body does the talking. You get a gut feeling or an unexplained physical sensation, such as a dry mouth, increased heart rate or sweating. You are a sensor. You may also have heightened sensitivity to things you touch, taste and smell and be able to sense the 'vibes' of a place or what others are feeling.

Everyone is unique and all of us experience Akashic insight in different ways. If you know your strongest clair, it is highly likely that this is how insight from the Records will come through for you.

# Read and write

♦

You will need to keep an up-to-date Akashic Records journal or document to catalogue your impressions after each reading. It can be easy to forget the insights that come through. In addition, writing down your experiences will give you greater understanding of yourself and clarity about the Book of Your Life. A plain notebook will do, or you can create a digital document if you prefer to type. It doesn't matter how you choose to keep a record, just make sure you do.

Your Akashic journal can help you see how much progress you are making, what pathways for accessing the Records are optimum for you, and what is or is not working. You can reflect on those Akashic impressions later, ideally just before you go to bed. It helps to have a little distance from your reading, so you can be more objective when you review your notes.

Remember to date stamp the impressions that come through and describe them as fully as you can. Like a detective, you are gathering evidence from the Book of Your Soul and your journal will be a great learning tool, especially when reviewed in hindsight.

Chances are, the impressions, associations and insights you write down will be slight at first, but this is no reason to discount them. The more you discount them, the weaker they will become and the more attention you pay them, the stronger they will become. They may also appear incomprehensible, but do not worry if you don't understand them right now. That's why keeping a journal is so important, because the revelations may come in the days, weeks or months ahead when you start to see a pattern – or even glimpses of your future – emerging.

## TELLING THE DIFFERENCE

You'll need to tell the difference between genuine Akashic impressions and negative or wishful thinking. Note that Akashic wisdom:

- Will energize and empower you. It will raise you up and never accuse, criticize, diminish or demotivate you.
- Is unexpected, unusual and fresh. It will come out of nowhere and typically surprise you.
- Is calm and unambiguous. There will be no doubt or confusion about it.
- Doesn't stay in your head – it will encourage you to do something and take positive steps in your daily life.
- Will encourage you to focus on the present – what you can change in your life right now.
- Tends to be felt from your stomach or a specific area of your body, whereas fear strikes the entire body.
- Repeats itself gently until you get the message.
- Proves to be right over time.

# From preparation to practice

Assuming you have taken on board the important preparation guidelines in this chapter, you are officially ready for your first reading. Time now for you to move from preparation to practice.

In Part Two, you'll find six suggested Akashic Record pathways and I urge you to work through them all in order, as each one builds on the momentum created by the previous one. Then, once you've worked through them all, consult your journal and the impressions recorded there and decide which pathway offered you the greatest guidance and illumination. If one clearly stands out, you have found your Akashic pathway for now. Congratulations! This is the pathway that currently matches your energy vibration.

Don't worry if some of the pathways don't resonate. You are an amazing, energetic work-in-progress and the only way to evolve is to experiment constantly. Making mistakes is the best way to learn. Simply refocus your energy and attention on the pathway that plays to your strengths and notice and record any impressions with an inner smile.

Don't be tempted to immediately seize on just one pathway. Try them all, as each one will teach you something surprising about yourself. Methodically working through them will also send a loud and clear message to your Akashic Records that you are fully prepared, disciplined, curious about and receptive to their infinite wisdom. You're willing to go outside your comfort zone if necessary to discover your optimum Akashic pathway and enter a committed, long-term and deeply loving relationship with your Records.

You might achieve positive results with more than one pathway. If this is the case, work with these until one emerges as the clearer channel. It is not essential, but optimum, to have one specific pathway to access your Records. Moving forward, you want to concentrate fully on the information you receive in your reading, rather than the best pathway.

When you have performed your chosen pathway, wait and be receptive to whatever you feel, see, hear, sense, know or experience behind your closed eyes. You may need to sit for a while until anything comes through, especially if this is your first reading, and that is entirely normal. Patience is a virtue.

Be aware that your chosen pathway may change as the circumstances of your life alter, and you grow older and hopefully wiser. Always keep a keen eye on the pathway you are using and if you feel the Records are not speaking to you as clearly as before, it may be time to choose a different pathway. Simply return to that section of the book (see pages 74–149) and revisit the other pathways. You may find they yield different results this time in response to shifts in your energy vibration.

Once you feel you have access to your Records, you can then ask them a question (see pages 155–158 for advice on how best to frame questions in a reading), or you can simply enjoy the view and be open to whatever the Records feel you need to know.

You can also ask the Guardians of Your Galaxy – the angels and spirits eager to help you connect with your Records – either out loud or with your thoughts to help you understand the information. If you're in any doubt about its meaning during a reading, don't hesitate to ask your spiritual helpers for clarity.

And now the Akashic scene is well and truly set, it is time for you to learn how to do your first reading. Follow the template at the start of the next chapter and you have nothing to lose but everything to gain.

**TIME OUT**

Should you feel overwhelmed at any time by all the insights and suggestions as you work through this book, just take a deep breath and some time out. Stretch and yawn. Go for a brisk walk or have a drink of water. You can't do everything at once. One small step. One giant leap for your soul at a time.

PART TWO

# Discover Your Akashic Pathway

*Akashic Wisdom Unleashed:*
*Infinite knowledge is available to you. You don't need to create it. You just need to access it by asking for guidance with an open mind and heart. Avoid thinking about your ability or lack of it. Relax and allow the Akashic Records to do your reading for you.*

CHAPTER 4

# Guided Meditation

# Meditation: Finding a way in

Part One helped you become more familiar with the history and purpose of the Records and how they can reveal their endless love and wisdom. Part Three will explore what you can ask and what you can do when your Records are open. Part Two is the bridge between this knowledge and experience. It will show you how to access and open your Records. There are a number of effective techniques and none is better than the other. You simply need to find the best method for you.

Initially, your focus should be on successfully accessing your Records and becoming acclimatized to the energy-shifting altitude there, with feelings of respect and gratitude rather than asking a specific question. Once accessing them is more instinctive, feel free to bring on those questions. (Chapter 10 will explore the most effective way to do this.)

For now, concentrate on discovering the best method for you to connect to your Records and stay as open as possible to whatever they choose to reveal. This connection is more likely to happen when your brain is in an impressionable state and you feel deeply relaxed and calm in body and mind. You are naturally in this brain state just before you fall asleep and on waking. Sometimes it happens spontaneously in your daily life, when you have a eureka moment or intuitive hunch, or are in a state of flow when you're so absorbed in a task or thought that you lose sense of time.

One of the easiest and swiftest ways to consciously achieve mental and emotional receptivity to an Akashic reading is meditation. It is a tried-and-tested way for achieving the essential receptive but deeply relaxed state that is so conducive to receiving Akashic inspiration.

In the previous chapter you were encouraged to perform a short, daily, heart-centred meditation as part of your Akashic Record reading preparation. Now you're ready to build on that foundation and focus your daily meditation around the specific intention of moving from heart-ready to mind- and soul-ready. In other words, transitioning from one state of consciousness to another, from your regular everyday awareness to heightened Akashic energy vibration.

# Your first Akashic Record reading meditation

♦

There is nothing like direct personal experience, so when you feel ready to access your Records in a meditation for the first time, carefully follow the steps below:

**STEP 1** Find somewhere quiet and safe where you won't be disturbed and sit comfortably. Set a timer for how long you want to spend on your Reading. See pages 61–65 for guidance on the importance of planning and timing.

**STEP 2** Close your eyes and perform the *Wisdom of the Heart Meditation* on page 67 until you feel calm and your heart is beating rhythmically.

**STEP 3** Notice but don't interact with your thoughts and feelings. Then let this observational stance help you gain awareness of your consciousness existing independently of your body and mind.

**STEP 4** Tell yourself, out loud or in your thoughts, that you feel ready to read the Book of Your Soul. You are deeply grateful for whatever will be revealed and will remember it. Use your legal name when you make this request. For example, 'I [insert your name] respectfully request to see my Akashic Record. I am deeply grateful for whatever illumination from my past, present or future it will offer me.'

**STEP 5** Concentrate on the sound energy of your name and on the feelings of love filling your heart. Feel your energy vibration become lighter, quicker and freer.

**STEP 6** Visualize a large, ancient-looking book with your name on the spine and the ability to open itself to the page your Akashic guides need you to read or know now. This is the Book of Your Life where you can access all the information you'll ever need.

**STEP 7** If you can't form mental imagery (a common condition known as aphantasia), sense, feel or describe how you imagine your Akashic Record to look using words, either out loud or silently in your thoughts. (See also the gazing meditation advice on pages 86–88.)

**STEP 8** Alternatively, visualize a vast library with ancient pillars at the entrance and endless shelves of books and scrolls inside. If these traditional images don't resonate, visualize a screen and an app with your name on it or an Akashic search engine you can type your name into. At this point, you can place your Records in a magnificent setting – such as a grand library, temple or a hall – or view the Book of Your Life in isolation or in a modern setting. In truth, you can visualize it in any way you want, as it is your energy and intention that matter the most.

**STEP 9** However you choose to visualize, ensure your Akashic Record is an image surrounded by and filled with light and loving energy that brings you deep peace and joy and reminds you how worthy and precious you are. Notice all the details in your visualization and feel them with your physical senses, as this will help deepen your meditation.

**STEP 10** With your mind and heart wide open, visualize the book opening by itself to a specific page and receive whatever Akashic guidance flies from the pages. You may read words, see images, feel emotions, hear a voice, conjure ideas or just experience a deep sense of knowing. Probe for clarity if whatever comes first to your awareness does not make sense.

**STEP 11** When the time is up, slowly let your consciousness drift back into your body. Close the reading with feelings of gratitude and positive expectation. Open your eyes, stretch and yawn loudly to ground yourself.

**STEP 12** Reach for your Akashic journal and write down the time and date. Then record whatever impressions you received. Don't force them to make sense. Simply write down whatever came to you.

## A 20-MINUTE GUIDED AKASHIC MEDITATION

If visualization flows easily, you may want to try the guided Akashic meditation on the pages that follow. Record yourself reading the descriptive script on pages 81–83 on your phone or other recording device. Be sure to leave plenty of pauses between each phrase, so that the meditation lasts around 20 minutes. (Note: If you find it easier to hear me read the words with accompanying relaxing music, tune into Episode 3, Season 9 of my spiritual podcast *White Shores*).

Then find somewhere quiet where you won't be disturbed. Sit comfortably and hit the play button. Let your own voice – or mine – guide you to the Book of Your Life and a conscious living connection with your own soul.

I have used the imagery of floating with clouds in the guided visualization. You can change that to a sandy beach where the waves dance, or a lush forest path filled with green trees, singing birds and colourful flowers that leads you to a white marble temple glistening in the sun. Inside that sacred temple there is nothing but high buildings filled with stars and endless rows of books, one of which is yours...

Over time, you may want to write your own guided meditation script. It's a wonderful exercise in creative writing. For now, though, feel free to use this script until your Akashic vision becomes clearer and you feel inspired to create your own Akashic paradise.

## *Akashic visualization script*

You are about to enter a state of deep healing meditation. Make sure you feel grounded and comfortable in your environment, so you can relax. Sit with your back straight and ask your body to relax. Close your eyes and notice how your eyeballs naturally move upwards, as if they sense what is to come.

Move your awareness to your physical body. The temple of your soul.

Your body holds your emotions, beliefs, soul and your consciousness.

Breathe deeply.

Relax.

Relax more.

Relax deeply and feel calm and centred.

Form or feel the presence of a vision of a ball of white diamond light behind your eyes.

Breathe deeply from your stomach and feel no rush. Breathe in through your nose and out through your mouth.

Your mind, body, spirit and emotions are interconnected. The Universe is not just physical. It is metaphysical energy and you are at one with that energy.

Shift your awareness to the glowing ball of light between your eyes. Let it open your mind to higher dimensions of consciousness.

The Universe is infinite empty space and you are part of the Universe.

You are infinite empty space waiting to be filled with love, light, wisdom. Allow universal energy to slowly and gently fill you up.

Relax your fingers and join your thumb and first finger together on each hand to create a protective circle. Keep your fingers like this even if you start to feel pressure.

Visualize or think about yourself lying on a comfortable, soft and gentle cloud gently floating in the sky. Lying on this cloud infuses you with loving and healing energy. Feel the cloud relaxing every part of your body. Feel any worries, stress or attention leave your mind and be absorbed and feel supported and loved by the cloud. Drift into a deeper and deeper feeling of relaxation.

Count down slowly from 10 and know that when you reach 1 you will have gently shifted to a higher dimension and that access to the Akashic Records is yours.

Your awareness is now in the Akashic Realm. Feel warm and cleansing light flow through you as you open yourself up to the wisdom and wonder of the Records.

The Akashic Records are a timeless living library of all human intentions, emotions and actions. A record of everything that has happened, is happening and will happen. There is a Record there of the journey of your soul. It is waiting for you to open it.

Observe the place. See a white marble floor beneath your feet. The floor feels warm beneath your bare feet. The surrounding space is a misty white and just ahead of you is a white chair. Sit on the chair and make yourself comfortable. You feel welcome and relaxed.

Know that your intuition is ignited. Wisdom through just knowing is now yours. Sensing the glowing light and love filling up your heart, the time is perfect for you to set an intention to receive wisdom and guidance from your Record.

Out loud or in your mind ask to see your Akashic Record now. See a theatre or stage floating in front of you. Ask the stage to show you what your soul needs to know at this time. Let knowledge flow directly into you without interruption from your thoughts.

A scene is forming on the stage. Allow it to form. No questioning. Just observe whatever forms, actions and scenes take place. Tell yourself you will remember them. You may hear a voice. Listen.

Let your fingers and hands rest from their circle formation now. Wisdom and higher guidance have made their presence felt. You are at one with the Universe and in harmony with the powerful light around and within you. You are being enlightened and energized. Your intuition is being activated with self-awareness, self-love and self-belief.

Know that beyond this guided meditation you will continue to tap into this Akashic wisdom and insight will continue to come to you. This timeless library exists in a realm of love and there is nothing to fear.

Create an energy cord between your higher self now and your Akashic Records. Stay relaxed and still. Visualize or think about a cord or energetic spiral travelling through your spine, through your heart and now out through the top of your head, connecting you to the theatre or screen containing scenes from your Akashic Record. Feel connected now and secure and calm.

You now have all the timeless wisdom at your fingertips at all times. Slightly bow your head towards your heart. Express your gratitude and respect for the wisdom available to you. Thank the Akashic Records for the insight you have received.

Allow the stage and cushion to disappear and any other images to fade. Allow your vision to draw to a close. Appreciate with awe the beautiful white space you have been in and feel one, loved and at peace.

Now start to count from 1 to 10, returning to everyday perception when you reach 10. You are mindfully back in your body.

Direct your focus back to your body and breathing. Notice your eyes being closed and your lips touching each other. Allow them to smile. Gently shrug your shoulders, then let them soften. Stretch your arms and legs. Take your time and open your eyes when you feel ready.

You are still an open channel receiving wisdom. You are no longer a stranger to the knowledge and paradise of your own soul.

Spend a few moments reflecting.

Finally, when you are ready, reach for your journal to record whatever impressions have come.

# Whatever comes through

In the majority of cases, in your first reading the energetic guidance of the Records will not come through images, symbols, words, thoughts, voices or sounds, but a sense of knowing or gut instinct. Indeed, this is how most people, myself included, receive most of the guidance from their Records. This may feel vague and frustratingly elusive at first, but in fact that is its power because it will encourage you to question it and reflect on the meaning. When things are not obvious you ask questions and probe deeper.

A reminder again here of the importance of journalling. Committing any Akashic wisdom to words, whether spoken, written or thought, creates an energetic shift and deepens your connection to your soul. Words have an energetic power. The Records may be infinite, but this experience is always going to be personal and immediate for you, and when you don't understand what the Records reveal you will automatically find yourself asking questions. This is empowering, as asking questions – why and what energy is behind things happening in your life – marks the beginning of all self-awareness, personal growth and wisdom. The purpose of the Records is to foster your self-awareness and help you reconnect to the loving nature of your soul.

And, after you have written down your impressions, don't immediately try to decode them. Get back to the business of your day. You always have more life lessons to learn and more pages to fill in the Book of Your Life. The ideal time for reflection is the evening, when you have some distance from the reading and can be more objective.

Don't be impatient with yourself if you felt nothing at all come through. It is very early days yet. Keep on meditating daily with feelings of respect, love and gratitude. Don't force or strain, as this comes from a place of fear and any kind of fear shuts down your access to the Records. Simply double down on the preparation steps in the previous chapter and experiment with another approach. And try the gazing pathway on pages 86–88. It is especially helpful if you are struggling to visualize.

## CASE STUDY: WHEN A SHIFT IS REQUIRED!

Lara was a recently divorced mother of two. She felt hopeless about her life. She had married young and put her dreams of becoming an artist aside to concentrate on her family. She couldn't point to a specific reason for her marriage breaking down. They just both knew they no longer wanted to spend the rest of their lives together.

But when her husband moved out, Lara slipped deeper into apathy and indecision. Although she continued to be a loving mother, she couldn't muster the energy to do anything positive. She told me she felt empty and irrelevant.

When I first met Lara, her cynicism about her chances of happiness felt energetically draining. It did not surprise me that this energy was making her feel stuck and distancing other people from her. I encouraged her to consider an Akashic Record reading in the hope that it would create an inner energy shift and inject some self-love into her heart.

I suggested she took a few days to prepare for that reading, to help her feel more receptive to any Akashic guidance that came through. After just 24 hours doing the preparation work, she got in touch to tell me that during the *Wisdom of the Heart Meditation* (see page 67) she felt inspired not just to write in her Akashic Record journal but also to draw in it. This was the first time she had drawn anything since the birth of her first son. I encouraged her to continue to draw in her journal whatever came through in her readings moving forward.

A few months later, Lara messaged me in a state of excitement. She had submitted some of her meditation-inspired drawings to a mind-body-spirit publisher. They had asked her to be the illustrator for an oracle pack. Better still, this career development had happened after her depression began to lift and she started to draw for pleasure again.

# Gazing

♦

If you have tried an Akashic Record meditation and found the experience frustrating, because you can't visualize or picture images in your mind's eye, and describing the Records to yourself in words or thoughts doesn't cut it, here's an illuminating alternative. You should give it a try even if you can visualize successfully.

Choose a picture in this book, ideally an artist's impression of the Akashic Records, and gaze at it. Don't stare; just gently look at it and, as you do, breathe slowly and deeply and drink in every single detail. Commit it to memory. Take as long as you need and enjoy the immersion experience. Then, when you feel ready, pick up your journal and write down, or draw if you feel so inclined, what you can remember of the picture. You aren't trying to create a work of art here. No one will see this but you. Just let your memory and vision go wild. And if you feel like adding your own details, all the better.

You can seriously enhance this gazing practice by playing slow, relaxing music – ideally music you adore that gives you goose bumps – at the same time. Shakespeare got it right. Music is the food of love and love is an essential ingredient for an Akashic reading, along with gratitude. The reason music can be such a rewarding Akashic pathway companion is its proven ability to reduce anxiety and bring inner harmony, a state of mind most receptive to Akashic wisdom. As you listen, your logical mind searches for patterns in the musical notes and sounds, leaving your intuition free to daydream. For once, your logic and intuition are not at war or trying to cancel each other out, but walking side by side doing what they do best.

And if when you listen to music you feel inspired to dance, don't hold back. Losing yourself in a piece of music – and letting your body do the interpreting alongside your thoughts – unites your body, mind, heart and soul in an energetic synchronicity and creates a matching vibrational rhythm. A flowing connection to the Records can spontaneously open, allowing sudden Akashic inspiration to surface.

# Looking up

The natural world is a liberating place to meditate and connect to the energy of your Records. A spot of cloud-watching and/or star-gazing can raise your vibration, enabling you to open the Book of Your Soul. It will also remind you that you're a part of the infinite love and wisdom of the natural world and that the clouds and stars are made of the same stuff as you. Everything in the Universe is energetically interconnected. You are part of something greater.

Cloud-watching or star-gazing could not be simpler. It will also feel familiar and comforting – remember lying in the grass as a child and watching the clouds form shapes above you, or trying to create a face or image by connecting the stars.

Fnd somewhere safe outside where you can lie down, sit or stand for ten minutes or so. Place your journal by your side. Then when you feel comfortable, look at the shifting shapes above you, but do not stare directly at the sun. Don't intently stare, just gently gaze upwards and notice any patterns, symbols or images forming above you. Observe any thoughts or feelings that come to you when you are gazing, but don't interact with them in any way. Take note too of any internal insights or knowing that comes. When your gazing time is up, reach for your journal and write or draw any impressions that flowed through you.

And don't stop at meditating under the clouds and the stars. Nature is such a rich resource for your Akashic work. You can meditate when you admire a glorious sunrise or sunset, or when you gaze in awe at the full moon, a shimmering lake or the miracle of a flock of birds. Awe is a feeling that never fails to elevate your vibration.

Remember too that your fellow human beings are a part of the natural world. A sign you are progressing with your Akashic work is that you will increasingly start to see yourself as part of the bigger shared picture of life. You will sense that raising your energy vibration isn't just going to empower you, but also play its part in raising the collective energy of the whole planet.

From now on, endeavour to see inner beauty in others and, whenever you can, consciously choose to think, say or do something to help raise their energy vibration. This can be something as simplc as smiling, saying 'Thank you', holding a door open, or feeling empathy and compassion. Notice how your words and actions really can light others up energetically – and the place to see that energy first is in their eyes.

## Your eyes have it...

So, perhaps the perfect meditation aid to use at any time to help you connect with your Records is a mirror. Hold the mirror in front of your face and gently focus your gaze and loving appreciation on the intricate colours and deeply mysterious beauty of your eyes.

And your eyes are not just the windows of your soul; they are also one of your defining physical characteristics, a part of your body. When you gaze into your own eyes, you're connecting with yourself in both soul and body. Your body is a sacred temple for your soul, which is why the chakra work pathway follows on naturally in the next chapter.

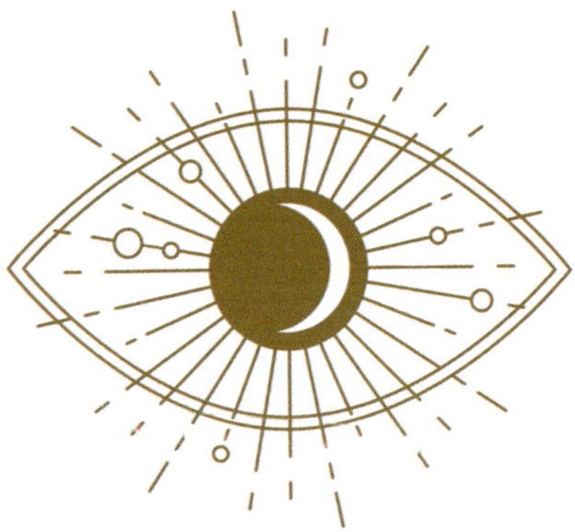

CHAPTER 5

# Chakra Work

# The power of energy work

Meditation can help you access the Book of Your Soul, using the intuitive power of your mind and its ability to transcend space and time and fly you directly to the Akashic Realm. However, it is important to remember that your body is also an intuitive force that you can tune into – and you can access your Akashic Records through certain energy centres in your body, called chakras.

Even if meditation proves to be an effective medium for accessing your Records, you're still encouraged to experiment with energy work as well. There is always a risk with meditating of getting trapped in your head. As powerful as visualizations and meditative experiences are, without positive actions to follow through or a hefty dose of practicality to validate those intentions, they remain in the realm of possibility. Energy work is grounding because it is felt and experienced in your physical body, reminding you that you're a physical being.

You are on this Earth for a reason. If you don't act on Akashic wisdom, it isn't going to change your life for the better. Just as you naturally judge someone by their actions – what they do rather than what they think or say – it is the same with your personal and spiritual growth. Your Akashic Record may contain the energy of your thoughts and words, but the power to turn the pages and move forward always lies in your actions – it is these your Akashic guides watch over most closely and value the most.

In essence, energy work encourages you to follow through when you have received Akashic wisdom. To be a person of actions, rather than words. To walk your talk. Show rather than tell.

Before showing you how to access your Records through the chakra energy centres in your body, a few explanations are required.

# What are chakras?

The word chakra originates from the ancient Indian Vedic tradition and means 'wheel'. A chakra is usually depicted in art as a spinning spiral of light. The spinning action both attracts and repels energy. The symbol of the chakra is known as yantra and resembles a lotus flower, with the petals representing the energetic qualities of the chakra.

Chakras are believed to be the portal between your physical body and your energy or spiritual body. If that interface is jammed, the resulting energy block can have a negative impact on your holistic well-being and limit your ability to access your Records. However, when your chakras spin freely, energy flows effortlessly, enabling access to the Akashic Realm.

## The magnificent seven

There are believed to be hundreds of chakra points all over the human body, but there are seven major ones and each of those chakras has different energy speeds, qualities, colours and associations. All seven chakras work synergistically, supporting the flow of energy between them. However, each individual chakra can draw energy towards and also outside itself, connecting your body to the energy outside and creating an energy field, known as an aura.

### THREE LOWER VIBRATING CHAKRAS

The Base chakra is located at the bottom of your spine between your legs and is associated with the colour red. It is about trust, safety, stability and physical health. If the Base chakra is blocked or imbalanced, this can create feelings of fear, insecurity and anxiety.

The Sacral chakra is located a little below your belly button and is associated with the colour orange. It is about sexuality, passion, pleasure and creativity. Signs of blockage or imbalance include creative blocks and intimacy and dependency issues.

The Solar Plexus chakra is located just above your belly button and is associated with the colour yellow. It relates to your confidence levels, willpower and inner strength. Signs of imbalance include low self-esteem, poor concentration, and stress.

### FOUR HIGHER VIBRATING CHAKRAS

The Heart chakra is found where your heart is and is associated with the colour pink or green. It is all about love and compassion. Imbalances include a lack of empathy and relationship problems.

The Throat chakra is associated with the colour blue. It expresses communication, clarity, inspiration and truth. Blockage signs include problems with expressing yourself and nervousness.

The Third Eye chakra is in the middle of your forehead and is associated with the colours navy and indigo. It is in charge of your intuition, insight and imagination. Signs of imbalance include indecision and a lack of clarity.

The Crown chakra is at the top of your head and is associated with white and violet. It is all about finding enlightenment and your connection with universal energy/the divine. Signs of imbalance include loss of purpose, apathy and depression.

## FEEL YOUR POWER

Rub your hands together vigorously. Place them together in the prayer position and slowly move them apart a centimetre or two. Then bring them back to the prayer position. As you do this, you may notice an invisible energetic power pushing your hands apart or pulling them together. This is your chakra power at work.

# Introducing your Soul Star chakra

The seven main chakras are the most well-known and commonly used in energy work, but when it comes to accessing the Records you need to familiarize yourself with a chakra point that doesn't get enough attention. It is the eighth chakra – known as the Soul Star chakra. It is located above the Crown chakra and rests above you like an invisible halo. It is believed to be the entrance to the Akashic Records and the place where information flows in through your Crown chakra to all the other chakras. It is often symbolized by a glowing star of bright white and regarded as the gateway of divine love and spiritual wisdom.

Your Crown chakra must be spinning freely and healthily before you can access your Soul Star chakra, so focusing on releasing energy blockages to your Crown chakra is vital. And because all the chakras communicate with each other, the healthier the other six chakras are, the healthier your Crown chakra will be and the clearer your connection to your Soul Star chakra and your Akashic Record. In short, blockages in any of your chakras, whether higher or lower, will have a negative impact on your ability to access the Records, as they work synergistically. Tend to them all.

There are things you can do to help balance your chakras and boost your holistic well-being, and the good news is all these things also help you access and read your Records with greater clarity. It's a win-win.

Operating from a place of love and gratitude can instantly help balance your chakras, as can respecting your body and mind by eating healthily, exercising regularly, getting quality sleep, keeping your mind stimulated and watching your stress levels. You can also gift yourself the transformative power of trust.

Before you perform the chakra work pathway on pages 98–100 to access your Records, set the intention to start noticing these seven power points in your body more. You can also start looking out for the eight chakra colours in your daily life, as they could all be Akashic signs.

Chakra balancing work can offer tremendous insight into your physical and emotional well-being. But it can sometimes be hard to stay balanced when life gets stressful. This is where reading your chakras from an Akashic perspective is so helpful. With your Records open, when you scan your chakras for signs of imbalance you can see the bigger holistic picture and the reasons contributing to any issues. This will inspire you to take practical steps to ensure energy blockages don't return and ensure the way to your Akashic Records is kept clear.

## CHAKRA SCAN EXERCISE

This book has repeatedly stressed the importance of your belief or intention when accessing your Records. This is because energy goes where your thoughts go. Don't believe me? Try this little experiment. Think of someone you love deeply. It could be a family member, partner or your pet. Notice how thinking of them makes you feel physically and emotionally. Do a quick chakra scan and observe any sensations in specific areas of your body. Then think of someone you don't like or distrust. Notice how just thinking of them impacts your chakras and overall feeling of holistic well-being. This proves the power of belief and how the Universe mirrors it for you.

## CASE STUDY: WHEN A SHOT OF PERSONAL POWER IS NEEDED

John was always a glass-half-empty person and proud of it. As an accountant he felt that being realistic was an asset but, although talented at his job, he never seemed to get noticed or promoted. I met him a few months after he had been made redundant. He had applied for hundreds of jobs but had not got past first interview stage. The feedback he received from recruiters was that he ticked all the boxes but lacked a certain spark, or they didn't feel the chemistry for their team was right, or his answers to their questions were not convincing.

During his redundancy, John's mother had a stroke. He became her carer during her recovery and on top of that was also visiting his grandfather every day, as he was showing all the signs of cognitive decline. He did go on dates, but hadn't found anyone he felt passionate enough about and preferred his own company. He was a keen cricket fan and a long-term member of his local cricket club, playing as often as he could. His social life revolved around that club and the matches they organized. Given his aptitude for the game, he had often been asked to captain the team but always declined, fearing he didn't have the leadership potential. John was a heavy smoker and even though his father had died of lung cancer he smoked two packs a day.

Listening to John's story, it was obvious there were serious energy blockages. I applauded him for having the courage to be open-minded enough to consider an Akashic reading, given his preference for logic. I encouraged him to tune into the wisdom of the Akashic Records through chakra work, as I sensed his passion lay with his cricket prowess. When we discussed what impressions came through, he told me that he felt a sense of emptiness in his Solar Plexus and without warning tears flowed down his cheeks. He told me he could not remember the last time he had cried.

I encouraged him to cry if he wanted to, as it would help him release the victim energy that was creating feelings of insecurity, guilt and anxiety. With his Solar Plexus imbalanced it was difficult for Akashic wisdom to flow through him, because he felt undeserving of good things even if they did come to him. Healing his Solar Plexus became a priority, given that it is all about personal power.

We discussed practical ways to boost his Solar Plexus energy and sense of personal power. The first step was to stop smoking. The second was to face his fear and become the cricket captain he deserved to be. The third was to tell his mother and grandfather that he was going to sort out a care plan for them, as he could not be everything to everyone.

The Akashic reading was outside his comfort zone, but had spoken clearly to his logical mind. In a matter of weeks, he stopped smoking, spoke to his family about sharing the caring load and became captain of the cricket team. With those key changes imprinting themselves on his Akashic Record and shifting the energy he was attracting, he was offered a well-paid job as an accountant for a company that ran retreats for busy executives.

John also stopped feeling something was wrong with him because he enjoyed his own company. He understood why. An additional Akashic reading showed him a past life where he had lived a blissfully solitary and mostly silent existence as a Buddhist monk!

# How to access your Records chakra-style

Wisdom and energy from the Akashic Realm can flow into your body with your chakra points acting like receptors. You can tune into the energy vibrations of your chakras to see if the vibration matches the information you are seeking. In other words, you can identify and release blockages and find answers and healing. Each of your chakras will gift you with a message to help you manifest your soul's higher purpose.

## Chakra exercise

**STEP 1** Lie down on your back or sit with your back straight and your hands resting gently on your knees.

**STEP 2** Close your eyes, take deep breaths and let your eyeballs lower behind your closed eyes, indicating that you are looking within.

**STEP 3** When you feel fully relaxed, state out loud or in your thoughts your legal name, and your intention to respectfully access and read your Akashic Records by tuning into your chakras.

**STEP 4** Focus on your Base chakra at the bottom of your spine. Notice how that part of your body feels. Think of the colour red and its associations. Consider how safe, secure and grounded you feel and if those are lacking, allow feelings of security to flow into you via your Base chakra.

**STEP 5** Move your attention to your Sacral chakra below your belly button. Think of the colour orange. Consider how passionate you feel. Allow creativity to flow into you via your Sacral chakra.

**STEP 6** Shift your focus now to your Solar Plexus chakra above your belly button and think of the colour yellow and how confident this area of your body makes you feel. As you breathe in, allow self-belief to flow in via your Solar Plexus chakra and, as you breathe out, let go of self-doubt.

**STEP 7** Bring your attention to your Heart chakra now, in the middle of your chest, and think of the colour pink. Consider how loving and forgiving you currently feel towards yourself and others and allow feelings of unconditional love to flow into you via your Heart chakra.

**STEP 8** Shift next to your Throat chakra and think of the colour blue. Consider how effectively you are communicating with yourself and others right now and allow assertiveness to flow into you via your Throat chakra.

**STEP 9** Move your attention upwards to your Third Eye chakra between your eyebrows and reflect on the colours navy and indigo and associations with those. Consider how imaginative and intuitive you feel right now and allow inspiration to flow into you via your Third Eye.

**STEP 10** Allow your focus to move to the top of your head and your Crown chakra. Think of the colours purple and white and allow your consciousness to flow directly into the bright white colour of your Soul Star chakra hovering above your head. The wisdom of your Akashic Records is now available to you.

**STEP 11** Sense enlightenment flowing directly from the Akashic Realm and funnelling through your body to all seven chakras.

**STEP 12** Perform a body scan, starting at your toes and feet and moving up to the top of your head. If you sense tension or blockage in any area of your body, breathe deeply into the area and feel Akashic loving energy rushing towards and all over it.

**STEP 13** When you feel your chakras have aligned, take a deep breath and thank your Akashic Records for raising your vibration and bringing you inspiration, balance and healing.

**STEP 14** Open your eyes and take a few moments to gather and ground yourself. Then reach for your journal and write down any sensations, feelings, thoughts, images, sounds or inspirations that came to you.

## Record what you experienced

Most important of all, be sure to record which chakra brought you what information. For example, if your Akashic Records want you to build your self-confidence, that data would likely be sent to you when you focused on your Solar Plexus chakra, which is associated with your sense of personal power. Anything to do with practical application and the importance of self-care would be sent through your grounding Base chakra. Brainstorming inspiration might come through your Sacral chakra. Insight about the current quality of your relationships would reveal themselves through your Heart chakra. Issues with honesty and communication would speak through your Throat chakra, and so on.

## Stay consistent

Unblocking your energy through chakra work is proven to boost holistic well-being. It is also a fantastic way to access and read information from your Records. As with every Akashic pathway, consistency is key. You need to set aside time each day to do it, even for just a few minutes.

Ideally, you should do a chakra session at the same time each day. Early morning or in the evening before you go to bed are when your brain is most receptive to receiving Akashic guidance, but you need to find a time that works best for you. When you do it matters less than ensuring you actually do it and continue doing it.

And when you practise a chakra session, be aware that, although you are tuning into Akashic wisdom through the wisdom of your own body, the power of your intention still plays a crucial role. The sacred prayer pathway introduced in the next chapter doubles down on the transcendent power of your intention to help connect you directly to your Records.

# CHAPTER 6

# Sacred Prayer

# Do I have to pray?

♦

Prayer is perhaps the most well-known and widely discussed and used pathway to successfully accessing and reading your Akashic Record. But as effective as prayer can be, please don't feel it is the only way. You are encouraged to experiment with this pathway according to the guidelines offered here, but if you feel that prayer isn't something you want to commit to on a daily basis, rest assured the other five pathways in this book can be just as enriching.

## What is prayer?

The word 'prayer' has religious associations because the primary meaning of the word, according to standard dictionary definitions, is typically along the following lines:

*Prayer is a deliberate act of worship that seeks communication with the sacred or a holy deity – God, the gods, the transcendent realm. It takes the form of a solemn request for help or an expression of awe and gratitude. Prayer is found in all religions in all times and can be a sacred collective or personal ritual utilizing various forms and techniques.*

But there is another non-religious meaning for the word: an *earnest wish, intention or hope.* This spiritual rather than religious meaning will be the context for the use of the word 'prayer' in this chapter.

A number of studies suggest that praying for hospital patients can have a subtle healing and life-affirming effect, meaning it should perhaps be the first rather than last resort during times of personal and collective crisis. You already know this to be true – doesn't it feel good when someone tells you that you're in their prayers?

# Say a little prayer for yourself

As well as praying for the benefit of others, you can, of course, pray for yourself. And this is what you'll be doing when you recite a sacred personal prayer to help you access your Records.

Praying brings intention, structure and clarity to your thoughts and hopes. You are letting the Universe know your desire, so there is no confusion. We live in a universe of interconnected energy and your thoughts and words create an energy vibration. By stating what you want, you are allowing the law of like-energy seeking like-energy to get to work.

If you think this sounds like the power of positive thinking or manifesting, you wouldn't be wrong. Yes, it is the law of attraction as popularized by million-selling books like Rhonda Byrne's *The Secret*. Prayer in the defining sense of being an earnest hope, intention or wish could well be described as manifesting.

You can recite an Akashic Record prayer silently with your thoughts, but it is far more empowering to say it out loud. Speaking rather than thinking words further raises their intensity and vibration, and this is especially the case with the Records, where sound travels without resistance and the energetic vibrations of sounds play a potent role in creating your reality. But which prayer should you recite?

## Which prayer to use?

The Pathway Prayer developed by Akashic Records author and scholar Linda Howe, PhD, is considered the easiest and most empowering prayer for gaining entry to this sacred place. The prayer is perfect for beginners and consists of two parts: an opening and a closing prayer, so it can be used for grounding and returning to everyday awareness afterwards, too.

The opening prayer is just three stanzas longs and requests the help and guidance of the Master, Teachers and Akashic guides. The closing prayer is a few sentences of gratitude. The opening prayer refers to the Holy Spirit of God and the closing prayer ends with the word Amen, which may not be ideal if you're not Christian or religious. Howe suggests inserting your legal name whenever the personal pronoun me or myself is used and to say the final line of the opening and closing prayer – 'The Records are now open/closed' – out loud to add formality.

The Pathway Prayer in its entirety can easily be found in book form or online, but you might want to experiment with the suggestions overleaf first, as following or copying others isn't always optimum when it comes to Akashic Record work. The Book of Your Soul is unique and any prayer you recite should match that uniqueness. And do bear in mind that the text for the Pathway Prayer was created in 2009 by Howe. Prior to 2009 people successfully accessed the Records, either by using the power of their own prayers or through other means.

Overleaf, you'll find a template prayer that I created based on my expertise in this area. It is my gift to you. Like the Pathway Prayer, you can choose to use it, but I suggest you play around with the wording a little and add a dash of your own creativity and vision to make it your very own personal Akashic prayer. Recite the prayer in your thoughts and out loud several times until it feels natural. Doubt will likely invade while you're reciting, but don't let that faze you, as it is part of the process while you adjust to a different level of consciousness.

## PRAYER TO OPEN THE BOOK OF YOUR SOUL

Read this prayer three times and after the first reading insert your legal name in the brackets to replace the personal pronouns 'me' and 'myself' in the second paragraph.

*In this beginning, and in this precious moment, we greet*
*the divine energy of the Universe and earnestly request*
*the inner strength and wisdom to know what is true*
*and for our highest good and the good of others.*

*Lords of the Records, please help me [insert legal name] open my*
*mind and heart and see myself [insert legal name] clearly and*
*fully through the light, love and clarity of the Akashic Records.*
*Help me [insert legal name] to live and share the meaning,*
*wisdom and compassion the Akashic guides want me to know.*

*The Akashic Records, and the Book of My Soul, are now open.*

*So it is.*

## CLOSING PRAYER

*My sincere gratitude to the Lords of the Akashic Records*
*and my Akashic guides for their higher perspective*
*and infinite love and compassion for my soul.*

*My endless gratitude to the divine energy of the*
*Universe for the knowledge and healing it is always*
*bringing me and everyone and everything.*

*The Akashic Records, and the Book of My Soul, are now closed.*

*So be it.*

# Timeless prayers

Once you start utilizing the power of prayer to help you access your Records, don't be surprised if you start feeling the holistic benefits. You may find yourself craving more time to pray and self-reflect afterwards, and that is a positive sign.

You may also want to prelude your meditation and chakra work with an Akashic prayer recited out loud to help raise your vibration. For example, before you begin chakra work you could ask the Lords of the Records to allow your body to become a portal for energy to flow within and through. Before you do an Akashic meditation you could respectfully ask your Akashic guides to give you permission and accept your request to access and read your Records.

The Akashic prayer template on the previous page is based on both ancient and modern forms of Akashic prayer. At the risk of repeating myself, I urge you to imprint your own creativity on the wording. Overleaf are a few other short prayer suggestions that you could personalize:

**A PRAYER FOR HEALING**

*Akashic forces of light, please help me receive clearing information and energy from my Records, so I can heal the damage done to my soul. Let light heal my wounds and fully restore my body, mind, heart and soul.*

**A PRAYER FOR HAPPINESS**

*Pure and blissful beings of Akashic light, help me to remember that happiness is my birth right. Let me see joy and meaning in my Records and only the highest good in myself and in everyone and in everything.*

**A PRAYER FOR REASSURANCE**

*Ancient forces of Akashic wisdom, let me see in my Records what I need to know right now to release my fears and doubts and help me find the courage to leap into the unknown if need be.*

**A PRAYER FOR LOVE**

*Dear Lords of the Records, allow the power of unconditional love to flow through me when I read the Book of My Soul and let that love stay with me and attract those into my life who love, value and support me.*

**A PRAYER FOR CLARITY**

*I call upon my Akashic guides to help me understand the Book of My Soul with clarity. Help me clear away any confusion clouding my thoughts, feelings and vibrations and let the energy of those confusions melt away into space.*

**A PRAYER FOR RESPONSIBILITY**

*Forces of light, help me release blame for any past, present and future wrong that my Records choose to reveal to me. Let me understand that I am the creator of my own divine experience and that this responsibility is mine and mine alone.*

**A PRAYER FOR PURPOSE**

*Divine Lords of the Records, allow me to see my Records and to be guided by the highest vibrational good. Let me know that whatever is revealed is for my highest good and in the direction of my purpose, on purpose.*

# Repeat after me

If prayer isn't your thing, affirmations are a good alternative. Repeating positive intentions or statements to yourself can help rewire your mind, making it is easier for you to connect with the wisdom of the Akashic Records. Affirmations can also be used to promote holistic healing and self-love. They interrupt the negative thought patterns blocking your mind and replace them with life-affirming ones.

Affirmations are typically spoken rather than thought. Saying something out loud several times helps your mind process what you're saying as absolute truth, as the words don't just come from your thoughts but also your voice, giving them double the energy and conviction.

Your mind believes what you repeatedly tell it with your thoughts. It doesn't know the difference between opinion and fact and is extremely suggestible, especially first thing in the morning and last thing at night when it is in a relaxed theta brain-wave state. The brains of very young children are mainly in theta, which is why negative messaging to the young is extremely damaging. Those messages quite literally shape their growing brains. (The unlived lives of parents and other carers can cause so much damage to children.)

The good news – the empowering news – is that whatever your age, you can consciously choose to rewire your brain with repeated affirmations.

And twice a day you have an unmatched opportunity to access your Records and use the information there to change your life for the better. First thing in the morning when you wake up and last thing at night when you're about to go to sleep, repeat the following Akashic affirmation, or something similar that resonates better with you, out loud three times. Make sure the statement is in the present tense. This helps you to believe it is true and happening for you right now.

*I transcend physical boundaries, and I can connect to the wisdom of my soul in the Akashic Records anytime I want.*

If you feel embarrassed doing this because you share a bedroom, do it somewhere alone. The important thing is to say it proudly out loud. Going out of your comfort zone and surprising yourself is what Akashic Record work demands. The more you change how you think and feel, the more you raise your energy vibration and the easier it is to access your Records.

You may sometimes want to look in the mirror when you repeat your Akashic affirmations, or repeat them silently with your eyes closed. Find what resonates best with you and, as with every pathway, stay consistent. For example, repeat your affirmations three times every morning, lunchtime and evening. You may want to write your affirmations down too, put sticky notes in visible places or change your phone lock screen to an affirmation image.

It is not necessary to repeat your affirmations hundreds of times or in a ritualistic way. It is quality, not quantity, that matters.

### JUST SAY OM!

The meaning of the words in an affirmation is their power, but it is the sound that carries the power in a mantra. In the ancient Indian yogic tradition, mantra means a 'thought that liberates and protects'. It is a thought or word said out loud to help attune your mind to Akashic consciousness.

The vibration created by the sound of a mantra is more important than the word itself. Chanting that sound over and over again in your thoughts or out loud will attune you to the energy frequency of that sound and raise your vibration accordingly. Perhaps the most widely used mantra is *Om* (pronounced ah-uu-om), believed to be the endless sound of the Universe. By chanting *Om*, you attune yourself to this energy and become harmonized with yourself, the Universe and the Akashic Realm. You can chant mantras any number of times, but 108 is believed to be a spiritually significant number. Try writing 108 dots in your journal and crossing them off as you chant – it is deeply calming.

# The force of words and sound

Sound, like energy, travels without resistance in the Akashic Realm which is why prayer, affirmations and mantras, if used consistently and infused with the power of your belief, can be highly effective, immediate and efficient ways to open your Akashic Records and connect to the infinite wisdom waiting for you there. They can also complement your Akashic meditation and chakra work and bring deep peace, direction and illumination into your life.

## CASE STUDY: WHEN PRAYER IS THE ONLY ANSWER

Mindy never thought of herself as a spiritual person. A much sought-after website designer, her days and nights were filled with brainstorming visions and creativity. She was in a long-term relationship and there was talk of buying a house and starting a family. In the eyes of the world, she had it all, but she couldn't understand why she increasingly felt empty and as if she was going through the motions. She longed for her life to have meaning and purpose.

One of the self-help books she bought introduced her to affirmations. She found herself whispering one of the affirmations to herself – 'I am living a life of deep meaning' – and immediately felt a shift from the inside out. She liked how vibrant it made her feel and for the next couple of weeks, whenever she felt that familiar emptiness returning, she repeated the affirmation several times in whispers.

Following the feeling and the inner power it gave her, Mindy decided to go deeper in her research and started to write down her own affirmations and get more and more creative with them. Not only did she feel rejuvenated, but she also noticed that her friends began to seek out her guidance. Then her partner had an affair and her relationship ended. She lost faith in herself and doubt crept back in. She struggled to believe in her affirmations and felt her inner spark fading.

It was at this point that Mindy and I came into contact. Given her interest in affirmations, I encouraged her to read out loud Max Ehrmann's famous serenity prayer (you can find it online by typing 'Desiderata' into a web browser) and to consider using the power of prayer to help her open her Akashic Records. She urgently needed to see beyond the practical and material to the deeper spiritual meaning of her life.

Within days, Mindy understood that the power lay not in the words of her affirmations but in the truth of her being. She naturally embraced prayer as her Akashic signature pathway. Through several readings she moved closer towards self-acceptance and an understanding that her life was an endless journey of self-discovery, learning and growing from change and challenge. This process of evolution was where her meaning and purpose was to be found.

When her ex decided he had made a mistake and wanted to come back, she realized she had moved on and that a relationship was not essential to her happiness. She had found within herself a resilience she didn't know she possessed. She continues to live her life to the full and is a spiritual inspiration for both herself and others.

## CHAPTER 7

# Dream Reading

# Your soul never sleeps

Until this point, your Akashic pathway work has focused on activities you can do during the day. But your consciousness and ability to connect to the Akashic Realm does not vanish when you fall asleep at night. This is because your soul remains wide awake in the wonderful world of your nocturnal dreams.

Every night, your night vision offers you a priceless opportunity to transcend logic, reason, time and space and catch a tantalizing glimpse of your Akashic Records. Hopefully, after reading this chapter, going to bed will never have felt more exciting.

This epic journey to help you discover your preferred Akashic Record reading is a deeply personal process. It may take time, discipline and patience and a whole lot of practice, but you are worth it.

Please don't become demotivated if you are diligently following the guidelines and aren't getting clear results yet. Keep an open mind and heart and believe that the information you need from your Records is going to come to you in the right way when you're ready. And it may already be coming to you every night while you're sleeping. You just haven't been noticing or paying enough attention – until now.

## Night vision

Your nocturnal dreams can be a simple and powerful way to help you access and read your Records. Whether you recall them or not, brain scans show that you dream at least five or six times every night and the symbols, messages and sensations of your dreams can offer a wealth of Akashic insight into your past, present and future potential. All you need to do is recall those dreams and write them down. Keeping a dream journal, or incorporating your dreams into your Akashic Record journal, will help you track your progress and keep a record of your night vision over time.

# While you are sleeping

♦

You already know how helpful meditation can be for accessing your Records. The Dalai Lama once said the best meditation is to sleep and what happens when you sleep? You dream! You enter a different state of consciousness where there is no sense of logic, time or space, just infinite possibility, and many believe that the dreaming mind has direct access to the Records.

The old adage of sleeping on a problem is spot on, because being asleep allows you to reflect on your waking life from a non-material perspective. I believe that dreams are the most common but also most neglected way to access the Akashic Records. Each time you wake up with a dream on your mind, feel deep gratitude. Wisdom from the Records is making itself known to you. Even if you don't understand the meaning of your dreams, they are a powerful reminder that there is more to you than your body and a part of you is able to transcend linear time and space.

Scientists don't know for sure why we dream – it isn't to rest as is commonly thought because our bodies and brains remain active when we're asleep. But they do know that if deprived of the REM (rapid eye movement) stage of sleep, when most dreaming occurs, we suffer anxiety and swifter mortality. Perhaps, then, the reason we sleep is to dream. Indeed, the majority of sleep scientists and experts now agree that the symbolic language of dreams brings important items for our personal growth to the surface and that regular dream recall is a sign of an active brain and holistic well-being.

## Dream power

Your dreams are data from the Akashic Records and can offer you brainstorming insights, healing, out-of-the-box perspectives and deep understanding of the bigger picture of your life. Think of them as a symbolic reflection of the current energy vibration imprinting itself on your Record. This puts you in a powerful position, because if you don't like what you see or feel in your dreams, making changes in your waking life can help you course-correct. Dreams connect you to your Records, showing you the unconscious hopes and fears currently being recorded in the Book of Your Life, so you can work through issues in your waking life and discover hidden creativity in finding solutions. You may also find that writing down your dreams every morning opens the Records for you, as it connects you first thing to your intuition, the door to your Records. Even nightmares have a cathartic and healing effect, because when you wake up you have faced your fears or glimpsed a potential future, and you can now move on or away from them. Think of nightmares as transformative gifts from the Akashic Realm – your dreaming mind's attempt to heal you, just as a fever is a sign of your body healing.

# Dream time

When understanding messages from your dreams, note that most are symbolic, but some will offer glimpses of past and future lives. Time-travelling night visions tend to have a more vivid and realistic feel than symbolic dreams, which are usually like disconnected fragments in a music video. Both are gifts from the Akashic Realm and of tremendous value for your personal and spiritual growth. You may also experience psychic dreams, such as telepathic dreams (you know something you can't possibly know), lucid dreams (you know you're dreaming when you are dreaming) and dreams of Departed Loved Ones, angels and spirits. These messages from your deep subconscious may be the clearest and most direct channel to the Akashic Realm.

If you don't think you've ever had a psychic dream, you probably have but either could not recall it or dismissed it as chance. Perhaps you met a departed loved one or dreamed of living in a different time and place. Or perhaps you dreamed about something and a day or so later aspects of that dream played out in your waking life.

Dreaming your future is known as precognitive dreaming. When you are dreaming and your unconscious is unleashed, you encounter all aspects of your past, present and future selves. There may well be precognitive aspects to every dream you recall, and by keeping a record of your dreams, you will start to see how they comment on and foreshadow your waking life. They may often predict something that appears trivial – for example, you dream about a squirrel and the next day you see one crossing your path – but your dreaming mind is drawing your attention to this moment and the intersection between your dreaming and waking life for a reason. Let this déjà rêvé inspire you to reflect on whether the choices you're currently making are truly in your best interests.

Don't panic if your dreams are often anxiety-themed. Dreaming of something negative doesn't mean you are doomed. It just means that if you continue to think, feel and act as you currently do, this is where you are likely headed. Remember, the future is not set. It is created by your present and you can change your present in a heartbeat.

## CASE STUDY: WHEN A DREAM INTERVENED

Gary got in touch with me to share a precognitive dream. He believed it had saved his life. In that dream he was driving down an unfamiliar road. He passed a small church and came to a sharp bend. Before he had a chance to slow down, the headlights of an oncoming car appeared on his side of the road. The car was speeding and collision was inevitable. He woke up sweating and shaking. It felt as if he had actually been there.

It took a while for him to shake off memories of the dream, but after a few days he had forgotten all about it until he found himself driving down a road to visit a new client. It was a road he had never driven before but it wasn't really unfamiliar. He had driven it in his dream. Things got really weird when he saw the small church that had appeared in his dreams and the sharp bend in the road just after that church. It was exactly as it had been in his dreams.

In that moment he knew he needed to slow down and not drive around the corner at the speed he usually would. As he slowed down, a car came hurtling around the corner, but because Gary had been driving more slowly than normal, he could swerve away from a head-on collision in good time. Seconds later, a police car followed in hot pursuit. The police car had not been in his dream but everything else had: the road, the church, the sharp bend and the speeding car.

Gary was left in no doubt that the dream had given him a heads-up and saved his life. Since that seminal dream, Gary has diligently kept a dream journal. I introduced him to the Akashic Records and explained that his dreams can connect him to his Records and past, present and future versions of himself.

# Any dream will do

Symbolic dreams are no less valuable than precognitive ones. They help you understand yourself better and self-awareness is key to unlocking the wisdom of your Akashic Records. You might also find that when you open your Records, regardless of which pathway you choose, impressions may present themselves in symbolic form. Learning how to decode the symbols of your dreams can help you decode Akashic symbols, because the principles are the same.

Now your attention has been drawn to your stunning night vision and its ability to directly channel Akashic wisdom to you every night, there are three essential things you should do. You need to set the intention to dream and then you need to recall and write your dreams down (see pages 122–123), so you can reflect on their meaning (see pages 124–125).

## Setting the intention to dream

Your mind believes what you repeatedly tell it, so if you keep telling yourself you don't dream, or that dreams are meaningless, that is what you can expect. As the previous chapter showed, you can turn that around by repeating affirmations or positive statements, especially when you are most receptive just before you fall asleep.

Before going to sleep tonight, look at your pillow as if it were a mirror and repeat out loud: 'Tonight my dreams will reveal my Akashic Records to me and in the morning when I wake up, I will have clear dream recall.'

Believe in this statement and think or say it with a sense of trusting expectation and joy. Know that what you tell yourself in the minutes before sleeping will be stored in your unconscious, where it will influence your dreams. Make this intention to dream your Records every single night and then sleep on it.

Again, if you feel slightly ridiculous talking to yourself, that is good. Taking yourself less seriously can help you connect to your Records in your dreams. Think about it. In your dreams the only thing you can be certain of is craziness.

# Dream recall and tracking

You may have trouble recalling your dreams, but there are simple things you can do to remedy this.

Taking your dreams seriously and thinking about them as a potential source of illumination during the day will increase your chances of dream recall. Your dreaming mind needs your attention and trust in it again. If your waking life is stressful, dream recall may suffer, as the material world has become too dominant, so carve out time during the day for meditation to create mood-boosting inner balance.

Make sure your bedroom is a sanctuary and get enough B vitamins – these are the dream-recall vitamins and found in bananas, carrots and leafy green vegetables. Nourish your creativity and intuition by reading novels, admiring art and listening to music you love. Your dreaming mind draws inspiration from what you think about and do during the day.

Get into the routine of putting a pen and paper or audio recorder beside your bed, as a visual reminder of your intention to dream and write down those dreams on waking. Before going to sleep, set the intention of visiting your Akashic Records in your dreams and recalling those dreams.

On waking (ideally without an alarm, as these create dream recall-diminishing stress), keep still with your eyes closed for a minute or so, as any movement will divert your focus to waking reality and the subtle world of the unconscious can't compete with that. If nothing comes to mind, perhaps reflect on a previous dream from a few nights before, to activate the intuitive part of your brain where all dreams are stored. Check in with your body to see if any dream memories are stored there.

Then, as soon as dream images, feelings and sensations bubble to the surface, write them down in your dream journal. Don't wait until you have brushed your teeth or got dressed, as those memories will slip away. A few key words will do. Let the details go and focus on the bigger picture. Be sure to write dream memories in the present tense and forget about handwriting or grammar. Also try drawing memories from your dreams. If there is no recall, write down how you feel on waking as that will have been inspired by a vision in a dream and it might ignite recall. And don't worry – it's normal not to have dream recall all the time. Just trust that your dreaming mind has been working positively on your behalf each night and ask it to talk to you the following night.

Be sure to record the date in your dream journal and then leave the interpretation until later in the day. You need some distance so you can be more objective when decoding the meaning. You may find as you go about your day that dream memories suddenly appear. This is most likely to happen when you're doing something routine that keeps your conscious mind busy – such as showering or walking. It temporarily suspends dominance, allowing your dream memories to make their presence felt.

You may want to record your dreams in your Akashic Records journal, or alongside a diary of your waking life, so you can see how your dreams are commenting on and sometimes foreshadowing your waking life. This will also help you see that your dreams are better understood in combination with other dreams. Don't fall into the trap of focusing on one particularly memorable dream. You should see your dreams as a long-running series that you need to tune into night after night to understand the narrative. For this reason, decoding the Akashic wisdom revealed in your dreams is always best done in hindsight.

### DREAM BIGGER

Once dream recall and tracking are underway, you can take a step forward. Before you go to sleep, you can ask your Akashic Records to offer information regarding any questions you have, or ask them to send you a dream in which you experience what you want to happen. This is helpful because dreaming about something suggests, on a deep unconscious level, that you believe it to be possible. And what you believe to be possible is the magnet in waking life that attracts good things your way.

# Decoding your dreams

Your dreams will share their Akashic wisdom through the language of symbols, puns, associations and metaphors, like a night artist or poet. In other words, look for deeper meanings and associations beyond the literal interpretation. For example, the symbol of a rainbow is associated not with the weather but with optimism. Many of us have lost the instinctive ability of our ancient ancestors to understand symbolism. Time to rediscover this, as it will also be invaluable for understanding information that comes through in an Akashic reading when you're awake.

On rare occasions, dreams can be literal. For example, if you dream your teeth are falling out, is a trip to the dentist overdue? Or you may find yourself living a previous life or glimpsing a future one. However, the vast majority show symbolic stories and visions of the state of your inner world, your unconscious. Every symbol and scenario points to something that you urgently need to know about yourself and your waking life. Unless you dream of someone you are emotionally intimate with, when other people appear in your dreams, they typically represent aspects of yourself that you need to face, acknowledge, express or heal.

A great way to start decoding the meaning of a dream is to ask: 'What does this mean to me personally?' You can consult dream dictionaries, but bear in mind they offer universal interpretations which may not apply to you. Your personal response is key. For instance, if you dream of a cat and love cats, it will have a very different interpretation for you than it will to someone who is allergic to them.

When a dream symbol surfaces, use the free-association technique. Write down the first thing that comes to mind. Then brainstorm what Akashic wisdom the dream is trying to tell you about yourself. You'll know when you have the correct interpretation because you will feel energized and positive. If an interpretation drains or disappoints you, then it is not from the Akashic Realm. The correct interpretation will always uplift, energize and also surprise and teach you new things about yourself.

Any kind of motion or vehicle in a dream suggests the direction your life is heading in. Notice if the elements of water (emotion), fire (passion), earth (grounding) or air (intellect) are dominant. Colours have messages too, as do locations, and pay attention to your role. Are you in the dream or observing it? How do you feel about that role? Do you want to change it?

If a dream recurs, take this as a positive. The wisdom it is trying to impart is very important and the dream will stop repeating as soon as you understand it. But if you have a dream that you can't make sense of, please don't worry. Perhaps the dream was sent from the Akashic Realm to ignite your curiosity, creativity and sense of infinite possibility.

And if you have a nightmare again, don't panic. Nightmares are transformative warnings and gifts from the Akashic Realm, an incredible opportunity to course-correct. If you don't like how a dream makes you feel on waking, or an Akashic vision of your future self in a reading is alarming, your power is now. You can alter the likelihood of experiencing that feeling or that potential future manifesting by changing your current mindset.

### LET'S GET LIMINAL

The twilight states between waking and sleeping are called liminal states. You may become aware of images forming behind your eyes and those can be a source of insight and creativity from the Akashic Realm. You're not dreaming when in a liminal state, but it is a prelude to dreaming and you can experience colours, lights, images and sensations. What you observe can be a revelation direct from the Book of Your Life.

Naps are a proven way to boost concentration and creativity. Set a timer for around 15 minutes in the mid-afternoon. Lie down, close your eyes and watch what you experience behind your eyes without judgement and resist the urge to direct or interpret. When the timer goes off, write down and brainstorm whatever Akashic information you noticed.

## Get over yourself

Every time you ponder the meaning of a nocturnal dream or a daydream, you understand yourself better from the inside out and the better you understand yourself – both the positives and the challenges facing you – the less dependent you become on others 'getting you', because your priority is to 'get yourself' first. You don't feel the need to convince others of your worth. In this way, dreamwork is such a fun and empowering pathway to the self-awareness, self-respect and self-belief required to access and read your Records.

When you value both your night and daytime dreams as pathways to Akashic wisdom, you start to love yourself from the inside out and this is where all the healing and meaning of your life is found. But even though dreamwork is a simple and instant way to access and read your Records, it is not the only way. Perhaps one of the most thrilling things about dreamwork is starting to see that, although there are common pathways such as meditation and prayer, whichever one you choose, you are the common factor.

The Akashic Records are not somewhere 'out there'. They are an energetic force within you. The British romantic poet William Blake famously said he could see 'A World in a Grain of Sand' and, like Blake, you will start to realize that you can see the deep wisdom of your Records in anything, whether your eyes are wide shut in your dreams or wide open in your intuitive hunches – which is the pathway explored next.

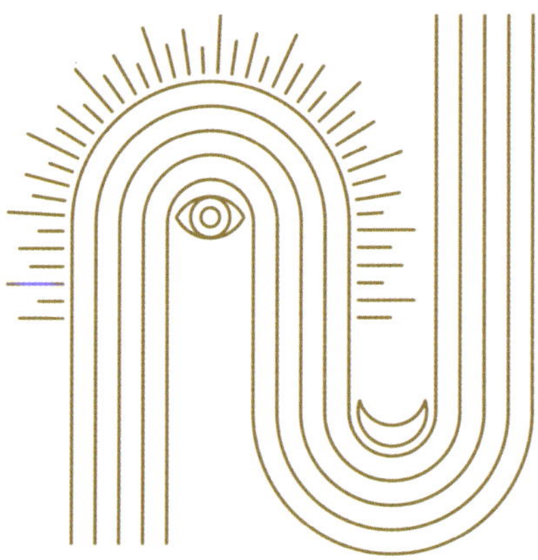

CHAPTER 8

# Intuitive Tools

# The power of intuition

It is possible to access your Akashic Records directly and instantly through your intuition at any time. Intuition is your deep inner knowing, a gut feeling, sixth sense or hunch that transcends logic. We all have an innate ability to sense energy within and around us. Intuition typically draws from memory, experience, learned knowledge and connecting patterns. It can offer swift insight and understanding and bypasses the need for reasoning. Studies have shown that this gut instinct can often be more accurate than overthinking. It can silence doubts and fears and lead you to making the best decisions for yourself. Not only can intuition help you access your Records, but it can also guide you while you're there, too.

You may be wondering, then, how intuitive insight differs from Akashic Record information. The difference is subtle but noticeable, as intuition tends to strike in the first person – for example, I feel or I know – and is very much in the present. Wisdom from the Akashic Realm is more observational and objective. You sense the bigger picture that transcends time and get a bird's-eye view of the present moment, the past influences that created it and the future potentials spiralling from it.

In essence, information from the Akashic Realm offers a deeper connection to the interconnected energy of the Universe and your place in that collective universe, but developing your intuition is a powerful way to access and read your Records. It is the channel or bridge connecting you to them.

Akashic wisdom may often present itself as symbols, as we saw in the previous chapter on dreamwork. Your intuition can help you understand those symbols and their associations and how they are commenting on your life. And perhaps most significantly, your intuition helps you trust the information from your Records even if it doesn't initially make sense.

# Count the ways

In this section, we have already covered four highly effective ways to develop your intuition, so you can directly access the Records.

Guided meditation and mindfulness practices can help quieten your mind, so it is calm and receptive to intuitive insights. Stress and anxiety are intuition roadblocks. Spending a few moments in stillness every day, focusing on breathing and observing your thoughts without interacting with them, can help you tune into your inner knowing.

Chakra work lets you tune into the gut instincts of your body, as this is a channel for intuitive insights. Notice any sensations in your gut and chest especially. Sacred prayer and affirmations can help you develop trust in the wisdom of your own voice, while dream reading encourages you to tune into your nocturnal intuition while you sleep.

Keeping an Akashic Record journal is also a way to strengthen your intuition. When you write down your dreams, thoughts and impressions, you start to recognize themes and patterns, which helps you gain intuitive clarity on them.

The best way to strengthen your intuition is to practise noticing and listening to it more during the day. It will speak to you through your dreams, feelings and the gut instincts felt in your body – typically your heart and stomach. Trust your hunches more and keep a record of the outcome. More often than not, over time, your gut instincts will prove to be correct. If they don't, try to discover why and learn from that.

The more you trust and act on your intuition, the more powerful it will become. So, next time you suddenly sense, feel or just know something to be true, take a moment to reflect. Your intuition is calling you. Use this moment of open-mindedness and creativity to directly access or channel wisdom from your Akashic Records. Don't doubt, fear or fight it. Relax and let that wisdom flow into you. Your intuition is like a muscle – the more you use it, the fitter and more flexible it becomes. You intuitively understand that, in your dreams and in quiet moments of stillness during the day, the wisdom you seek from your Akashic Records is already alive and kicking. It is present and living within you.

## FREE EXPRESSION TIME

A simple but powerful way to tune into your intuition and directly channel Akashic Record wisdom is automatic writing. This is similar to journalling in that you write down your thoughts, feelings and reactions but differs in that you set a timer and simply write without thought, however nonsensical the words may be. Don't try to make sense of the words. Think of it as doodling with words – then you're in a relaxed but creative state. You're bypassing the restrictions of your logical mind and letting your creativity and intuition express themselves freely.

When the time is up, read through what has been channelled and see if there are any associations. If it doesn't immediately make sense, that's fine. Keep an open mind and trust that – at a deep unconscious level – your soul is making profound connections and it will make sense in time when you're ready.

# Empower your intuition every day

♦

Whatever pathway you choose, remember your intuition will always be the door to your Records and your compass when you're in there. You are strongly urged to strengthen your intuition and your connection to the Akashic Records through daily practice, following the guidelines on page 129.

If you don't feel particularly intuitive, firstly change this irrational perspective and tell yourself that you are. This isn't wishful thinking. It is fact. Just as you dream every night, even if you can't remember your dreams, research shows that sixth sense (or intuition) is in your DNA. You have just forgotten how to tune into it. Reading and working through the exercises in this book will certainly help you ignite it. For additional support, you may find working with specific intuitive tools that offer a map to the soul, such as astrology or Tarot, can offer the reassurance you need that you really, really are an intuitive being.

*Note: When using any intuitive tool to help you access and read your soul's Records, always remember that the power is not in the tools, but in you. It is in the intention,*

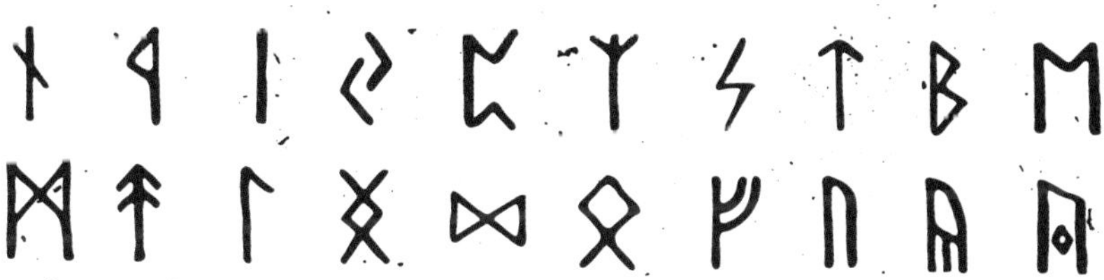

## CASE STUDY: WHEN A CLEAR, CALM VOICE IS NEEDED

*Content warning: Mentions sexual violence*

Cassandra had four older brothers. Her mother always told her that she was a miracle child, the daughter she had dreamed of. There was no shortage of love at home, but Cassandra struggled to find her identity and her voice. She failed to get promoted at work due to her lack of assertiveness and she tended to attract controlling partners.

Given Cassandra's loving family and an absence of trauma, it was difficult to understand why she didn't have confidence in her own voice. On her first Akashic reading using the sacred prayer pathway, she was unable to recite the prayer out loud. I suggested using Tarot cards and asked her to let me know which card triggered something within her. She told me that the Hanged Man spoke to her, but she wasn't sure why. The meaning became clearer the following morning. She recalled a dream in which she was a Victorian maid who was strangled by her employer when she screamed for help while resisting his sexual advances. The dream was so vivid and clear I told her it likely pointed to a past life where she had been silenced when she needed help. This gave her the understanding she needed for her fear of speaking up. She immersed herself in the Tarot cards and the journey of the soul they symbolically depicted in their art. It helped her understand that making sure her voice was heard was a natural part of life.

Every day she drew a Tarot card and asked her Akashic guides to help her use the wisdom of that card to communicate her emotions to herself and others. Her Akashic Tarot work reassured her that asking for help was not a sign of weakness, but a sign of wisdom and strength.

# Akashic Tarot reading

Before any Akashic Tarot reading, you need to form a respectful connection with the Tarot deck of your choice. This means spending some time researching the deeper, soul-level meaning of each card. The following provides a brief overview, so you can see if an Akashic Tarot reading resonates with you. If it does, you're encouraged to do more research on your own.

These illustrated cards date back to medieval times, perhaps to Italy. They're often thought to have occult or predictive powers that can only be interpreted by a professional reader, but they don't have magical powers and it's easy to learn to read them yourself. They can only show you a potential future: whether that comes to pass is entirely up to you.

There are thousands of different decks available, but I suggest you use the popular Rider Waite deck, which is widely recognized as the most compelling and with artwork that can speak directly to your soul.

## The Major and Minor Arcana

A Tarot card deck consists of 78 cards: the 22 cards of the Major Arcana, and the 56 cards of the Minor Arcana. Every card has an archetypal and symbolic meaning based on the depicted number, character or scene and offers an overview of your soul's journey.

The 56 Minor Arcana cards paint or repaint the events and details of your daily life. They are divided into four suits or elements, each with 14 cards from Ace to King, one more than traditional playing cards. The Wands represent fire and action, the Pentacles earth and the material, Swords air and thought, and Cups water and emotion.

The first seven of the 22 Major Arcana cards symbolize your interactions with the material world and others, cards 8 to 14 represent your feelings – your inner space and what your heart needs to know now – and cards 15 to 22 open your mind to the bigger picture and universal laws that may be impacting your present and future. Overleaf is a brief overview of the Major Arcana with key words.

**0 THE FOOL** symbolizes your inner child and new beginnings.

**1 THE MAGICIAN** symbolizes your control and mastery.

**2 THE HIGH PRIESTESS** symbolizes wisdom and teaching.

**3 THE EMPRESS** symbolizes your creativity.

**4 THE EMPEROR** symbolizes your leadership.

**5 THE HIEROPHANT** symbolizes practicality and tradition.

**6 THE LOVERS** symbolizes connection and coming together.

**7 THE CHARIOT** symbolizes your challenges and conquests.

**8 STRENGTH** symbolizes your resilience and control.

**9 THE HERMIT** symbolizes secrets and what is hidden.

**10 THE WHEEL OF FORTUNE** symbolizes transformation.

**11 JUSTICE** symbolizes balance and harmony.

**12 THE HANGED MAN** symbolizes crossroads and new perspectives.

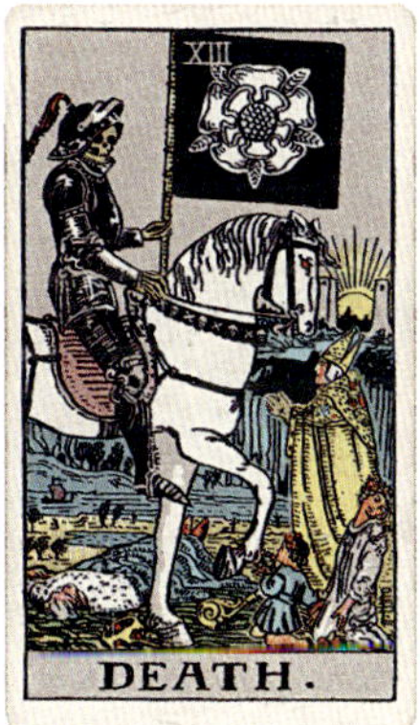


**13 DEATH** symbolizes rebirth.

**14 TEMPERANCE** symbolizes compassion and purification.

**15 THE DEVIL**
symbolizes temptation.

**16 THE TOWER**
symbolizes sudden change.

**17 THE STAR**
symbolizes optimism.

**18 THE MOON**
symbolizes concealment.

**19 THE SUN**
symbolizes revelation.

**20 THE JUDGEMENT**
symbolizes karma.

**21 THE WORLD**
symbolizes completion and opportunity.

# Pick a card, any card

✦

You might want to focus your learning on the Major Arcana first, as they're most strongly linked to the bigger picture or cosmic understanding of yourself and your life that an Akashic Tarot reading can reveal. Research their deeper meaning and when you feel confident, turn the cards face down and shuffle them. Then lay them all out face down in front of you and let your intuition guide you to pick one.

If you haven't got a Tarot deck, you may want to study the illustrations on pages 134–136 and see which Major Arcana card you're intuitively drawn to and what associations the images inspire in you. This may point you towards a richer understanding of the current energy of your Records. And, during the day, notice if the card you picked and the associations you made foreshadowed any events, situations or emotions.

Now familiarize yourself with the Minor Arcana. It might help here to do a daily card pull, where you pick one card at random from the deck and just think about the meaning of the card. If you do this first thing in the morning, you can keep it in mind throughout the day. This will really help you get to know the cards on a deeper level. You can learn the story of the card while also receiving guidance at the same time. Use an online or print Tarot guidebook to help you decipher the meaning until you feel confident enough to form your own.

Once you have chosen your Tarot pack, feel you've formed a personal connection with the cards and are familiar with the deeper meanings behind all of them, you can confidently use it to access your Akashic Records and open yourself up to the limitless wisdom and guidance waiting for you there.

## THREE-CARD READING

Using three cards is perhaps the best place to start, as it is so obviously in tune with Akashic Records, given it focuses on your past, present and future.

Simply shuffle the cards for a few minutes and, as you do, respectfully ask the Akashic Records to open for you. Then spread the cards out in front of you face down and intuitively pick three, one to represent your past, one your present, and one your potential future. Once you get to know the cards more, pick two cards for your past, two for your present and two for your future.

Remember, the purpose of an Akashic Tarot card reading is to unlock your higher self. It can show you where you are on your soul's journey, the past influences that explain this present moment in time, and what the future might hold for you, given your current energy vibration. You can consult a professional Tarot card reader for their perspective on what a reading means for you. But – and I'm aware this is getting repetitive now but there is power in repetition – your intuition only really pays attention and decides if you're ready to receive Akashic wisdom when you are the one doing the self-reflecting.

# Other systems

There are other tried-and-tested intuitive tools or maps to your soul aside from Tarot. If used with loving trust and self-belief they can also help you access and open your Akashic Records. Here are some systems that have given me encouraging results whenever I want to use props or a specific method to help me channel Akashic insight. If you need the structure these tools can offer, use them to connect to the Book of Your Soul. As with Akashic Tarot work, you need to research these systems first before using them as intuitive tools to help you open your Records.

### ASTROLOGY

This is the ancient science of charting the positions of the planets and stars when you were born and the 12 signs of the Zodiac contained within them. Each Zodiac sign has archetypal, or universally applicable, characteristics and potentials. The 'as above, so below' concept makes sense – the Moon rules the tides, for example, and humans are up to 70 per cent water. There is also a clear synergy between astrology and the Akashic Records, as both offer maps to your soul and a cosmic overview of your life, past, present and future. You can ask your Akashic Records reading to help you understand yourself and others better from an astrological perspective. Or ask it to reveal potential futures based on the the challenges and triumphs associated with movements of the planets.

### BIBLIOMANCY

One of my favourite intuitive tools because it is so simple and easy. You just need a book with plenty of pages of text that you feel connected to (hopefully, this one!) or even a sacred or religious text. Sit somewhere quiet, close your eyes, hold the book and ask it to tell you something you need to know from your Akashic Records. Open the book at a random page. Keep your eyes closed and put your finger on the page. Then open your eyes and read where your finger took you. Read the text and allow your inner psychic to interpret it as a sign.

**CRYSTALS** See pages 142–149.

### HUMAN DESIGN

This is a self-knowledge system that is a mashup of astrology, Kabbalah, personality traits, *I Ching*, quantum physics and the chakra system (see page 89–100) to generate an energetic blueprint called a Body Graph. This is a map of your genetic code, said to reveal your energy imprint and how you engage in the world, and has a strong synergy with Akashic Record work. Although it is currently enjoying popularity, unlike the other intuitive tools in this section, Human Design has not yet passed the test of time, having only been created in 1987 by Alan Robert Krakower who wrote *The Human Design System* under the pseudonym Ra Uru Hu.

### I CHING

The *I Ching*, or 'Book of Changes', is an ancient Chinese divination manual which interprets a series of hexagrams (symbols made up of six lines) – formed by tossing sticks or coins – to form answers to questions. Each of the 64 possible configurations represents a process in nature or human nature and is believed to indicate luck, growth or misfortune.

In many respects, the *I Ching* mirrors the timeless wisdom in the Book of Your Soul. It is a study of how your life changes over time. The theory is that understanding patterns and cycles of change can help prepare you both for the future and to make the right decisions. The life wisdom offered for each hexagram combination is deeply profound, as it is based on shared human experiences. For that reason, using *I Ching* can be a natural pathway to intuitively accessing your Akashic Records.

For over five thousand years, *I Ching* has been used in China to aid decision-making and prediction and is still used today. It can appear daunting and rather time-consuming at first. But, as with every intuition-boosting tool, the more you read about it and start using it, the easier and more natural it feels.

### NUMEROLOGY

This is the theory – dating back to ancient times and Pythagoras – that everything in the world carries the energy of, or can be broken down into, a number and that those numbers have certain associations and meanings. Understanding the energy vibrations of the numbers in your life, from the day you were born to your house number, can help you better understand both yourself and the world around you. When you notice them, numbers, especially repeating numbers, can also be interpreted as helpful spiritual signs or synchronicities. Repeating 1s – when you see 11.11 – are often thought to be a calling card from your higher self. Don't be surprised if, after reading this book, you notice 11.11 more often.

#### RUNES

These alphabet letters were used in ancient times in Northern Europe. The letters were originally inscribed on stones called runestones. Each stone has a symbol and each symbol a meaning. A runestone reading can offer intuitive insight into problems, or predict potential futures, in much the same way as a Tarot card reading.

#### SCRYING

This is the term most associated with fortune-telling. It involves looking at a reflective surface – a crystal ball, mirror, bowl of water, flame or even a thumbnail – and thinking of a question. The visual shapes and symbols you see can offer instant intuitive guidance or reveal a potential future.

#### READING TEA LEAVES

This works in the same way as scrying, but involves reading the shapes left by the tea leaves at the bottom of an empty teacup – in other words, tuning into your intuition.

### Your white feather

If you have ever seen the Disney movie *Dumbo,* about a small elephant with enormous ears, you'll know that Dumbo is gifted a white feather and told that it is magical. If he holds the feather tightly with his trunk, he can use his big ears to fly like a bird. To cut a long story short, Dumbo learns that he could fly using his big ears all along – the feather just gave him the belief to do so.

In many respects, all the intuitive tools and systems described here work in a similar way. They offer you something tangible to touch, hold or sense around which to structure your Akashic work and this can be helpful and comforting, giving your belief in the Akashic Records a focus point. And this is especially true when using crystals, the subject of the next chapter, as your chosen pathway.

# CHAPTER 9

# Crystal Companions

# Crystal power

♦

Crystals make inspiring and beautiful soul companions. Carrying one with you to boost your self-belief, placing one in your bedroom to boost dream recall, or holding one close to you to help unlock your intuition when doing Akashic readings can feel very reassuring.

I love and use crystals daily. They always boost my energy. When my confidence is low, I wear a carnelian bead bracelet. For self-love, I reflect on rose quartz and I place an amethyst, tiger's eye or moonstone on my bedside table for clearer dream recall. And when I do Akashic Record readings, I always make sure amethyst and lapis lazuli are close by.

These are just my personal preferences and there is a whole world of crystal power out there waiting for you to discover, wear, use and love. Much of the alleged power of crystals is linked to the energy vibration of your belief. Having stated that, some research suggests they emit certain energy vibrations that can help ease stress and light up your intuition. Find out more about the properties of each crystal, but always let your intuition guide you to the one that you feel most drawn to energetically.

**ESSENTIAL OILS**

You may also want to research the healing and intuition-boosting qualities of essential oils and spray them around, or use them on your person, when doing an Akashic Record reading. Find what essential oil feels right for you, but for Akashic Record work, I suggest starting with rose oil, clary sage, frankincense and sandalwood. And to boost your dream recall, try a relaxing lavender pillow spray.

# Using crystals to access the Akashic Records

♦

You need to feel balanced and at peace when you connect to your intuition and the infinite source of information waiting for you in your Records. Crystals can help you find inner calm and transcend the limitations of time in an Akashic Record reading. They have a long-standing relationship with spiritual enlightenment, including accessing the Akashic Records.

Ancient civilizations, such as the Egyptians, Mayans and Greeks, regularly used crystals in their spiritual practices. Shamans, priests and oracles believed certain crystals could help connect them to higher realms and bring healing and wisdom. They were thought to directly facilitate connection to the divine and were typically carved and polished and revered for their beauty and spiritual power.

## Choosing your crystal

Selecting the right crystal to complement and amplify your Akashic reading is crucial, so research their spiritual properties to find one that will be your most enlightening companion. The suggested Akashic crystals on the following pages will get you started, but there is a huge amount of choice out there. It doesn't matter if a crystal is endorsed or highly recommended by others, or even has a body of research behind it. What matters most is how the crystal feels when you hold it. Perhaps visit a crystal shop and see which crystal catches your eye – for example, how the colour makes you feel when you look at it. In short, research practically rather than in theory, and trust that your intuition will help you find your ideal crystal soul mate.

At the risk of repeating myself, you need emotional and mental clarity and to move beyond the interference of fear, doubt, your ego and the limitations of time to access and read your Records. This isn't always easy. Fortunately, there are crystals blessed with the spiritual properties needed to help you move through any interference and access your Records.

Crystal quartz

Amethyst

Selenite

To help you progress along the right lines, here are five crystals that have proven effective, which you might want as your crystal companion:

#### CRYSTAL QUARTZ

Also known as the 'master healer', crystal quartz is believed to have a pure, high-energy vibration to help you focus and avoid distracting thoughts, making it perfect for accessing the Akashic Records.

#### AMETHYST

Believed to have powerful, intuition-igniting properties that can deepen mystical insight and connect the material to the spiritual, amethyst is a friendly Akashic companion. It is also the dream recall crystal.

#### SELENITE

This crystal is renowned for its calming ability to remove mental confusion and unlock clarity. Seeing your truth and your own light as clearly and as objectively as possible is important whenever you access your Records.

#### LABRADORITE

Associated with transformation and psychic development, labradorite can also aid in the removal of self doubt. Working with its energetic properties can help open your mind and heart to the Records.

#### MYSTIC MERLINITE

This crystal is thought to be a mind- and heart- and therefore consciousness-opening crystal. If you are keen to recall past-life experiences, this may be the ideal Akashic crystal companion.

**OTHER CRYSTALS TO TRY**

Additional Akashic crystals you may want to experiment with include rose quartz (compassion and unconditional love), black tourmaline (staying grounded), lapis lazuli (emotional calm), fluorite (reading past and future lives), azurite (intuitive and psychic abilities), apatite (enlightenment), celestite (calming), jade (balance), tiger's eye (dream recall) and apophyllite (strengthen communication with Akashic guides).

And if you are co-ordinating crystal work with chakra work, red jasper corresponds to the Base chakra, orange carnelian to the Sacral, yellow citrine to the Solar Plexus, green aventurine or pink quartz to the Heart, blue angelite to the Throat, amethyst to the Third Eye, and clear quartz to the Crown.

## Preparing your crystal

Once you've chosen your crystal, cleanse it of any interfering energies imprinted by other people who may have handled it before you. Using a smudge stick or running water over it will suffice. Then you need to personalize your crystal and imprint your energy, belief and trust in it. Simply hold the crystal in your hand and place that hand on your heart, then your forehead, and send it your love and commitment to protect and cherish it always. You can also visualize a white beam of light travelling from the crystal to your forehead and heart. Finally, energize the crystal: depending on its properties, either leave it on your windowsill in the sunlight for a few hours or overnight in moonlight to absorb cosmic energy.

Mystic Merlinite

Labradorite

Moonstone

## Using your crystal

Once you've chosen, cleansed, personalized and energized your crystal, find a quiet place and sit down comfortably. Place your crystal in front of you and gently gaze at it as you open your mind and heart. Then hold it in your hand, close your eyes, take some deep breaths and trust that the energy of the crystal will empower your intuition and unlock the cosmic mystery of your Akashic Records. And be sure to take special care of your crystal between readings, so its energy stays clear and is reserved only for you and your Akashic Record reading work.

Labradorite

Selenite

## CASE STUDY: WHEN CRYSTAL POWER IS THE REMEDY

From an early age, Jo was drawn to matters of faith, but she became spiritual rather than religious and qualified as a primary school teacher. She got in touch with me when she had unpleasant dreams and felt inexplicably anxious. She was in a relationship, but it was an open one and it was clear she wasn't okay with this. She also didn't feel respected by her colleagues and the parents of her pupils and, on occasion, by the pupils themselves, even though she only had their well-being at heart.

I felt that meditation was the pathway for Jo to access her Records, but the results were disappointing. Then a friend gifted Jo a rose quartz bracelet, and she loved it. I told her about the spiritual properties of rose quartz and suggested she hold a rose quartz crystal close to her heart during her next Akashic meditation. This changed everything. The Records showed her past lives in which a lack of self-love was the dominant theme. She saw herself as a medieval prostitute, and in manipulative relationships. The crystal of unconditional love was helping her see that the root of her anxiety was her tendency to place the happiness of others above her own. Until she loved and respected herself, she would never feel loved and respected by others.

It took a while for Jo to course-correct as 'service before self' had been her soul's mantra for many lives. She didn't abandon it completely, but she realized there had to be a balance between care for herself and care for others. As soon as she understood the root of the problem, things fell into place. She ended her relationship, became better able to say no in her work and her life, and has never felt happier. Her rose quartz bracelet remains her constant companion.

# Follow your own clear crystal path

It can sometimes feel daunting clearing away external and internal distractions when you want to ignite your intuition and connect to the energy of your Records. It can also feel lonely at times. Crystals can be your self-loving companions.

Crystals can help raise your energy vibration, so you become a clearer channel for the Records. You can use them independently or to complement your Akashic meditation, chakra work, prayer and dreamwork, intuition and any other pathway to the Records. And when you have found the crystal of your Akashic dreams, don't restrict it to readings but carry it with you. Or choose a design that mirrors your soul and wear it as jewellery. Just make sure you wear your chosen crystal companion as close to your skin as possible, so its transformative spiritual energy can melt effortlessly into yours.

PART THREE

# Akashic Wisdom Unleashed

*Letting go of the demands and restrictions of linear time when you are in the Records releases you from dependency on others and material things for validation. In this place of trust, you know that you are always free to choose and live the life of your dreams.*

## CHAPTER 10

# Getting the Most Out of Your Akashic Reading

# Searching your Records

Regardless of the pathway you choose to access your Records, you'll notice an inner shift occurring when they open for you. You will gently move from a first-person towards a third-person perspective. You will know that you can be both an 'I' and a 'You' at the same time. You will leave behind linear time and dependency on material things for your validation and move from uncertainty to self-trust. And when this inner energetic shift from personal to objective, from doubt to liberation, has signalled that the Book of Your Life is open, what should you do?

Once you're in your Records, you can ask any question you want or request any guidance you need. Asking out loud has more power, because the sound of your voice resonates louder in the Akashic Realm than your thoughts. But if you can't raise your voice, whisper your question or write it down. It might help to compare this to an online search. You simply input or type in what you want to know and trust that technology will offer you a helpful answer.

It is fine to be specific. If you want to know about your past lives. Ask. If you want to know about your love life. Ask. If you want to know the future of a certain work situation. Ask. If you want to know about your health or the health of someone else. Ask. If you want to know the meaning of your life. Ask. You can go as deep as you wish.

Your Records will not show you all you want to know in answer to your questions, but what you *need* to know. You'll only receive information that is relevant to your current situation in life, what is happening for you right now in this moment in time. This is especially important to remember when asking about past or future lives. You need to trust completely that what you receive from the Records is what you're meant to receive. If it doesn't make sense yet, that's okay. We are not supposed to have all the answers to the mystery of our lives.

You can open the Records before you fall asleep to welcome in vivid dreams, or leave them open when working on a creative project, but when you're starting out, it is best to close them after around 20 minutes. You can use a closing prayer (see pages 105–106) or close them with grounding exercises such as stretching, stamping your feet, drinking a glass of water, and so on.

After your Reading, you must write down your experiences and date them in your Akashic Records journal. You may often find that the information you received has the feel of a nocturnal dream, so record the information the same way you'd record a dream on waking. Use key words and don't try to make sense of it.

Just as you shouldn't interpret a dream right away, do the same with your Akashic Records. Leave it for a few hours at least and then return to reflect on the meaning. And return to your Akashic Record journal every few days, so you can see a pattern emerging. Your Akashic journal, like your dreamwork journal (see page 115), is best interpreted in hindsight.

# What kinds of questions can I ask?

♦

Your Akashic Records can offer you a new realm of soul-level knowledge that you may not have encountered before, and this can feel overwhelming. You may not know what kinds of questions to ask.

You can do a reading without any question in mind and simply trust that your Records will show you the most relevant information without any preconceived notions to impede it. Indeed, I have encouraged you to take this unspecific approach when introducing the six suggested pathways (see pages 74–149). However, over time, you may want to ask the Records to be more specific and this is when the power of questioning – how you phrase your questions in particular – comes in.

Questions are more empowering than answers, because they can open your mind to new horizons and perspectives and help you brainstorm solutions. If you aren't sure what kinds of question to ask your Records, my advice would be to make them specific, open-ended and self-focused – so the question is centred around you and not someone else.

The Records don't work as well when you want a 'yes' or 'no' answer. They do not give definitive answers, as this would take the power away from your own choice. And the goal of any reading is to empower, not diminish you. If you do ask for a 'yes' or 'no' answer, you will probably get lots of questions to help you self-reflect until you find your own answer. So, for example, instead of asking, 'Should I stay in this relationship?' ask the records: 'What will my relationship be like if I decide to stay in it?' They also don't respond well to time specific, 'When will I ...?' questions. This is because your future is being created all the time by your choices in the present and any future you glimpse will exist in potential only.

In summary, the answers you receive will often be complex and given from the evolutionary perspective of your soul, to encourage you to reflect deeply, so you can make your own choices. The Records do not make choices about your life for you. That is your job.

Your readings can focus on your past, present or future potential and topics you could choose to explore include a huge range of issues, from how to boost your intuition and connect to your spiritual guides, to releasing abundance blocks and healing emotional wounds.

When deciding on your question, focus on one at a time and ensure too that questions are not based on linear time or start with the word 'when'. In the Records you can glimpse the journey of your soul across space and time and the rules of linear time do not apply. So instead of asking, 'When will I fall in love?' a more Akashic-friendly question would be: 'What can I do to become more receptive to romantic love?' Likewise, avoid introducing a sense of urgency or preconception about the timing and outcome by using loaded words such as 'soon' or 'likely'. And since your Records chronicle your past, present and future potential, decide which timeframe you want your reading to focus on.

The Records also don't respond well to questions starting with the word 'should', as that is asking the Records to make decisions for you. Switch the word 'should' to words such as 'why', 'how' or 'what'. For example, don't ask: 'Should I go for this job interview?' Instead ask, 'Is this job opportunity optimum for me right now and if it isn't, where can I find one that is?'

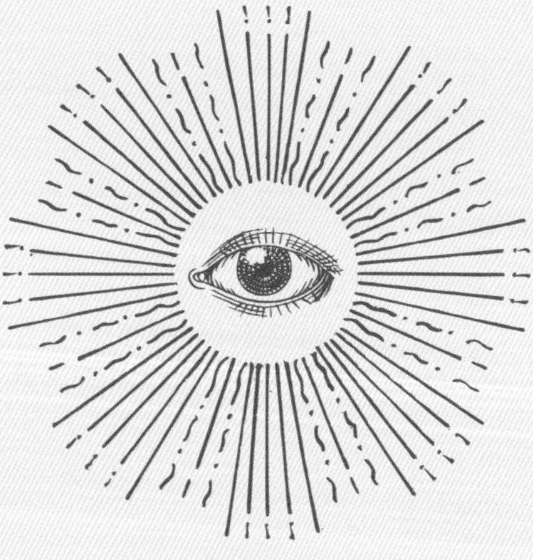

## QUESTION EXAMPLES

It can take a while to find the right approach to asking questions for maximum information to come through, but you'll soon get the hang of it. To help you get started, think short- rather than long-term and ask the Records questions such as:

- Where is optimum for for me to direct my attention and energy today?
- How can I approach today with gratitude and inner peace?
- What does my soul need me to learn today?

Then consider moving from the shorter to the longer term with questions like these:

- What must I learn from this relationship?
- Why is this person in my life?
- What negative relationship patterns must I now release?
- How can I attract more love and support into my life?
- What must I do to open up to the energy of love for myself and others?
- Is this job/career/work/project in my best interests?
- What is stopping me progressing in the workplace?
- What is limiting me financially and how can I change that dynamic?
- What is this current situation teaching me?
- How can I let go of anger/guilt/shame/fear/jealousy?
- What can I do to become more assertive?
- How can I find greater inner peace?
- How can I connect to my spirit guides more deeply?
- How can I become less reactive?

And from the longer term, you can take a leap of faith outside time into your past lives and future potential:

- What can my past-life career choices teach me about my current situation?
- Have I met this person before in a past life?
- What can my past lives teach me about any self-defeating attitudes and behaviours I need to release?
- What does the future look like if I stay in this relationship?
- How will staying in my current job impact me?
- Where is my future currently heading?

The above are just sample questions and you will notice how they typically begin with the words 'how' or 'what'? Try them out and see what results they achieve. Let them encourage you to create your own open-ended, soul-evolving questions. Allow any information and answers from the Records to filter through without judgement.

The goal of any question you ask your Records is to help you break negative patterns. To show what you can do right now to heal unresolved areas of your life, so you can let go of what no longer serves you and move forward feeling more empowered.

# What if you experience fear?

Fear has no place in an Akashic reading, as fear and love cannot coexist in your heart and soul. If you struggle to let go of doubt and fear, the best advice is to pause any attempt at doing a reading and to reread Part One of this book (see pages 24–73). It will remind you that the Akashic Records are yours and you are the one in charge here. You get to choose your thoughts, feelings and reaction. The Records exist for your benefit to help your soul evolve. You will also be reminded that anyone, including you, can learn to read the Records.

# What if you experience nothing?

♦

You may notice images, scenes, sensations, colours or symbols and metaphors for higher concepts that you need to take time to reflect on. On occasion, you may hear words or sounds, or you may sense feelings and energies. You may even get goose bumps. However, sometimes you may sense nothing at all and that's okay, as the Records are saying that you already know the answer to your questions. Or your answer could be in the silence, as your Records require you to find a deeper balance between the spiritual and the material in your waking life. It is possible the scales have tipped heavily towards the material and you need to spend more time daydreaming, walking in nature, listening to music, reading novels and admiring art to correct that imbalance and nurture your inner world.

Whatever the Records reveal or do not reveal, know that it is in your best interests and the information will come when you're ready. Chances are, you did notice something subtle in your reading, rather than total blankness. Perhaps it was a symbol or a feeling or a physical sensation? You probably didn't pay attention to it because it was not 'dramatic' enough. Time to flip the switch and trust every tiny thing that comes to you in a reading. Anything, however subtle, small or seemingly trivial, is a message. Follow it, write it down after the reading and trust your intuition, your inner voice or knowing.

Carry on doing your Akashic readings and writing down your messages. It can also help to revisit the advice about empowering your intuition on pages 128–131. The more you journal, meditate, trust your gut and tune into your inner voice, the clearer and clearer messages from your readings will be.

# Can you tune into dark or negative energies?

In a word: no. There is no negative or dangerous energy in the Akashic Records. If you feel any dark energies, this is your anxiety manifesting. You are strongly advised to stop any attempts at doing a reading and to ground yourself fully. Be sure to practise meditation and/or work on finding inner calm in your daily life before attempting another reading. Also consider doing some breathwork, cognitive behavioural therapy or shadow work to help you release those unconscious fears.

Remember, the Akashic Records can only allow loving and joyful energies into their Realm, because their purpose is to connect you to your higher self. Any energy that isn't blissful means you are not reading your Records. Negative energy has become a roadblock and closed the Book of Your Soul.

## Reading for someone else

You can only access someone else's Records if they have given you verbal and written consent. If you're a parent, you could do a reading for your child, but they need to reach adulthood before they can fully understand the concept of the Records. They also need to give you their permission.

It is a privilege to be asked to channel Akashic wisdom for someone else. Never pressure anyone to do a reading. Any hesitation is a sign they are not ready. If they are eager for a reading, bring none of your own judgements or expectations into the process and keep boundaries in place. You want the reading to be fun while also respecting the sacredness of the Records. Your objectivity is key. If you find yourself getting emotionally involved, stop the reading. Never share any information you gather with anyone other than the person you're doing the reading for.

Prepare yourself in the same way you would prepare for your own reading. Find somewhere quiet and safe. You can do the reading online but ensure your technology is up to speed and there are no connection issues first. If you are charging a fee, the price of a good haircut is the maximum you should charge – and discuss and resolve any payment issues before doing your reading. You can also ask your client to share the questions they want answered with you ahead of the reading.

Let go of doubt and fear and work with your chosen pathway to open the Records. If you use the prayer pathway, you need to say the person's legal name and not your own. When sharing information from the Records after your reading, ensure everything you say is positive and encouraging. If messages come through that you don't understand, simply share those messages with the person. Let them do the self-reflection and find their own answers. It their your role to interpret them, not yours. You are simply the Akashic vehicle here. Encourage them to learn how to do a reading for themselves. The direct personal approach is always the most relevant and powerful.

Reading for others may help improve the clarity of any readings you do for yourself. The more time you spend in the Akashic Realm, the more experience you gain. Even better, seeing others in the light of Akashic Record wisdom helps you become more understanding, loving and tolerant. And this movement to greater empathy is what every Akashic Record reading is pushing your soul towards.

# Your questions, your power

There is a school of thought that suggests crystal-clear clarity regarding the questions you want answered is always required before you access your Akashic Records through your chosen pathway. You state your question with confidence and allow yourself to drift into a meditative, receptive state, as if falling asleep into the Records. Then observe with gratitude whatever information you receive. When you've closed your reading, write down or record whatever has stayed in your awareness.

In my opinion, absolute clarity regarding questions can be helpful, but isn't always strictly necessary. It can also be incredibly beneficial to do a reading without any expectation at all and just to approach it with open-minded curiosity and a deep sense of gratitude and awe.

Every time you do a reading, whether you have a specific question or not, you connect to your soul on its evolutionary journey. You become more aware of your higher self and its unshakeable, loving connection to the wisdom and energy of the Universe, the source of all existence. You understand at a deep level that this knowing and sense of deeper meaning is your birthright and you deserve a greater understanding of your own infinite potential.

This sounds deceptively easy, but Akashic wisdom really is waiting there for you to trust, tune into and receive it.

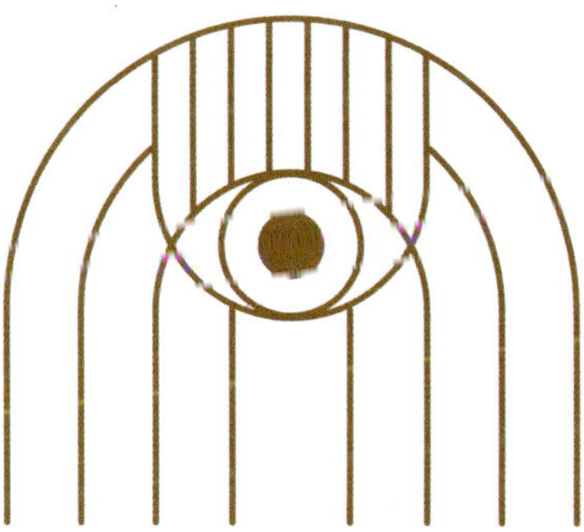

# CHAPTER 11

# Asking Your Guides for Help

# Should you ask for the support of a spiritual guide?

Given the Records are all about empowering you to make your own decisions, you may wonder if it is wise to ask for guidance. The short answer is, yes, if that support is spiritual. If any of the following questions resonate, you're already on the journey to self-awareness. Your guides can certainly help your soul discover the fulfilment of inner peace it is seeking.

- Do you want to know why certain things happen to you?
- Do you want to become a better version of yourself?
- Do you want to know how to overcome challenges in a positive way?
- Do you want to know how to feel more empowered?
- Are you invested in your personal growth and development?
- Do you think your life should feel simpler and more rewarding?
- Do you want to make better decisions?
- Are you seeking guidance for a problem?
- Do you want your life to have meaning and purpose?

If you answered 'yes' to just one of the questions above, you have everything to gain and nothing to lose from asking your guides to help you read your Records.

The first step is to decide which spiritual guide you want to ask. They need your clarity and trust ahead of your Akashic reading. Whichever one you select, they will respond with love and kindness. Find out how to decide on the next page.

# Which spiritual guides should I ask?

You can leap to the top and call on the Ascended Masters for support, those highly evolved spiritual beings who have previously lived as humans (see page 56). They have soul experience and know how to help you respond with love and kindness, whatever life throws at you. During their human lives, they made choices that helped them transcend karma and reincarnation and they chose to use their great wisdom to help human souls find self-mastery and inner peace. Or you may want to call upon the spirit of a Departed Loved One who always had your best interests at heart. This can be anyone you like, even a beloved pet. You can also call upon your own higher self.

However, when you start doing Akashic readings and are beginning the journey to self-mastery, perhaps the best guides to mentor you are your angels. Angels are pure beings of light who have not lived on Earth, but they watch over you constantly, see the bigger spiritual picture, and speak the language of unconditional love. What more could you ask for?

## YOUR ANGEL'S EXPERTISE

Before asking an angel to help you find your way in an Akashic reading, it can be useful to know their area of expertise. Review the list overleaf and take note of the angel that resonates most with your request or goals, then ask them for guidance by name on opening the Records. Each angel is accompanied by a specific colour and symbol, so if you see or sense that colour or symbol in your waking life, this could be a sign your angel is ready to work with you.

**ARIEL**, lion of God, is associated with the energy of courage, creativity, vitality and self-confidence. Orange, gold, white and pink are the colours for this angel and the symbols are lions or woodland animals.

**CHAMUEL**, seeker of God, is associated with the healing energy of reassurance and balance that can bring a sense of inner purpose and peace. Yellow is the colour and the symbol is anything made of gold.

**GABRIEL**, the messenger, is associated with the energy of speaking, teaching and honest, loving communication with others and also with yourself. All shades of blue are the colours and the symbols are books and lanterns.

**METATRON** is the leading Akashic Record angel, known as the scribe or 'Keeper of the Records', linking humans to the divine and associated with the energy of peace and clarity. Indigo, white and yellow are the colours and the symbols are cubes and repeating numbers.

**MICHAEL**, the warrior, is associated with the energy of initiative and acting with conviction. All shades of red are the colours and the symbol is a sword or spear.

**RAPHAEL**, the healer, is associated with the healing energy of love. Greens and blues are the colours for nurturing family connections, pink for loving bonds and white for healing a broken heart. Symbols for this angel include emeralds and bowls.

**URIEL**, the fire of God, is associated with the energy of inspiration and intuition. Colours are yellow, red, white and indigo and one of the symbols is fire.

# How to ask your Akashic guide for help

Once you've decided which loving spiritual being you want to accompany you and be your guide, healer and teacher, follow the meditation guidelines below.

**STEP 1** Find a safe, quiet space and set a timer if you need to. Sit comfortably and take some long, deep breaths.

**STEP 2** Visualize or sense a protective bubble of light energy all around you that no one can enter unless you invite them in.

**STEP 3** When you feel relaxed and calm enough, focus your conscious attention on your heart and feel it opening with profound feelings of love and gratitude.

**STEP 4** Call on your chosen angel or guide by saying their name out loud, writing their name down or thinking deeply about them and only them. Invite them to help you access the Records and guide you when there.

**STEP 5** Open your heart and your mind and allow yourself to let go of any concerns.

**STEP 6** If you have a specific question, ask your guide to help you find answers in your reading.

**STEP 7** Notice how you feel and if at any point you sense an inner shift or an awareness of yourself existing independently of your body, the energy of your guide is with you. You may also notice strong emotions, a higher energy or the sensation of being watched.

**STEP 8** This spiritual connection may be enough to open your Records spontaneously, but you may also want to perform your chosen pathway to access the Records, this time with the assistance of your Akashic guide.

**STEP 9** When your Records are open, notice whatever information comes through. Allow yourself to receive this – it may come as a symbol, image, word or sound.

**STEP 10** You may immediately understand the meaning, or need to wait until this becomes clear later.

**STEP 11** Close your reading, expressing gratitude to the Records and your Akashic guide for their assistance. Tell your guide that you want to keep this loving connection with them constant and that you're open to receiving their intuitive guidance at any time.
**STEP 12** Write down and date stamp your impressions in your Akashic Record journal.

Should you not sense the presence of your guide after calling on them, be patient with yourself. Keep practising and learning from every reading. It takes time to build a connection with your Akashic guides and sometimes, like the internet, even a strong connection can fade in and out. The best approach is to let go of expectation, stop trying to force things and simply trust that when you are heart-ready your guide will be there with for you.

And if you feel unsure whether you're sensing your Akashic guide, note that you are not sensing them. When in the presence of your Akashic angels, you will just know. The experience will be undeniable. And once that connection has been experienced several times, you may start to spontaneously feel the presence of your guides in your dreams and everyday life. You may notice their loving energy in nature, other people, animals or acts of random kindness, or hear their wisdom in a song, music or other signs.

Or you may stumble across a book like this which speaks directly to your heart and soul. Meaningful coincidences or synchronicities will become your everyday.

There is no right or wrong Akashic guide or way to ask for help. Trust your intuition and if you ultimately prefer to go it alone, that's fine too. Even when you don't ask for their support, rest assured, the Guardians of Your Galaxy are never far away. And remember, every time you access your Records, arguably the most empowering spiritual guide you encounter there will be your own higher self.

Your higher self does not float above you like a halo and it is not better than your personal or physical self. It vibrates at a higher spiritual frequency and is the part of you that connects you to the Akashic Records. It knows what is in your best interests and is skilled at helping you find your own answers and sensing the best direction for your future.

# Your higher-self Akashic handshake

In everyday life, your higher self and its natural ability to connect to your Records often gets roadblocked by the logic and reason of your conscious mind and your personal or physical self. You can achieve optimum results from your Akashic reading if your conscious mind and your higher mind are not at odds. This will be the case when doubt and fear creep in and there is absolutely no room for doubt and fear in an Akashic reading.

## Handshake exercise

This handshake exercise is designed to help your higher self and your conscious self reconcile and open a clear, harmonious channel, so your heart and mind are both open to Akashic wisdom. You're encouraged to do this exercise whenever you feel inner tension. It is also an ideal practice to perform before a reading, to facilitate the presence of your higher self when your Records are open, and afterwards to help you understand the information you receive.

**STEP 1** Find a quiet, safe space where you won't be disturbed. Sit comfortably. Take some long, deep breaths until you feel calm.
**STEP 2** Close your eyes and visualize, or describe in words or thoughts, your higher self. It doesn't matter how you imagine or describe this, because it is your higher self. It can be a rainbow, a superhero, a unicorn or anything or anyone you admire.
**STEP 3** Then imagine your conscious self as if you're standing across from it.
**STEP 4** Tell your conscious self that it has important and highly valued skills, such as discipline and direction and helping you take the necessary steps and form a plan of action after a reading.

**STEP 5** Tell your higher self it has important and highly valued skills too, such as intuition and creativity. It provides the vision for your conscious self to transform into reality.
**STEP 6** Tell your higher self that both sets of skills are necessary in a reading. You want the infinite wisdom of the Records to connect to your higher self, but also want to consciously notice, recall and make sense of any information that comes through.
**STEP 7** Ask your conscious self to ask your higher self to shake your hand and agree that each will use their own skills and let the other use theirs without interference. You may even want to put out one of your hands to shake your other hand to physically enact this invisible truce.
**STEP 8** If your higher self agrees to shake, that is great. If not, ask it what reassurance it needs from you before it will work in harmony with your conscious mind. Then give your higher self that reassurance.
**STEP 9** Open your eyes and write down in your Akashic Record journal how you felt and what you learned.

That's it. Your higher-self Akashic handshake is complete. Both your heart and mind have agreed to do what they do best and to work together for your next Akashic Record reading. Congratulate yourself on this state of union and your status as an official Akashic worker.

Over time, you may be able to shorten this exercise to a simple affirmation, stating that your conscious mind and higher self will agree to work together. You can also start telling yourself that you would like to listen more to the guidance of your higher self, not just in your readings but also in your daily life.

Tell yourself that you will listen more to your gut feelings and to the messages in your dreams in daily life.

Tell yourself you will take regular time out to self-reflect and meditate and write down any intuitive insights and impressions in your Akashic Record journal.

Tell yourself that you want to improve the communication channel to your higher self and all the wonders it can reveal. Setting this intention is important, because the more your higher self sees you taking it seriously, the more it will want to work with you and the stronger its presence will be in every single reading.

## CHAPTER 12

# Answers Across Time

# A lesson from literature

Even if you haven't read Charles Dickens's *A Christmas Carol*, first published in 1843 and never out of print since, chances are you know the plot. Spoiler alert here, but it could be the inspiration for *Akashic Records: The Movie*. It is about a deeply unhappy man called Scrooge who transforms his life overnight after being visited by the spirit of his departed colleague and then the ghosts of his past, present and future. He sees all the choices he made in the past, how they created his present unhappiness and the future of a lonely death towards which he is hurtling as a result. When he meets the final ghost – the ghost of 'yet to come' – he says it is the one he fears the most!

When Scrooge wakes next morning, thrilled to be alive, he feels reborn. Unwilling to live the desolate future that was foreshadowed, he decides to make immediate changes and alter that future. All ends well.

Interestingly, Dickens stated that the inspiration for perhaps his most famous work came to him in a dream and during frequent walks through the streets of London, suggesting that dreaming and mindful walking may have been his Akashic pathway. He may not have been aware of this, but his timeless narrative of a man transformed through mental time travel is not just a morality tale; it is an Akashic soul story. It shows we can all view our past, present and future in this observational way and make changes and find healing and meaning from the inside out.

# Travelling through your timeline

When you open up your Records, your past, present or potential future records may spontaneously appear. It is important to know the difference and to decide before a reading whether you want deeper insight about your past, present or future. Of course, past, present and future are interconnected on a timeless soul level, but you can get the best insight if you approach the reading with clarity about the timeline you want to view.

## Past Records

If you ask for insight about your past, your reading will likely focus not so much on your past in this life but on your previous lives, to help you identify recurring patterns and themes. Reincarnation is encapsulated by the belief that your soul needs many lives on Earth to find its purpose and that past lives can impact your present life through imprinted karma.

Your decision to access your Records could prove to be game-changing. It signals you now want to identify and understand the source of any karmic problems you've inherited, and such understanding is the beginning of all wisdom and growth.

For example, if your Records show you past lives where you had negative and limiting mindsets, this may show up in similar self-destructive tendencies in your current life. Or perhaps your past-life Records reveal a repeating pattern of relationship dysfunction or behaviour such as overspending or addiction that you need to let go of. Or perhaps they will explain why you have a fear of saying what you mean. Perhaps in a former life you were executed for your beliefs.

Don't panic if you view a former life where you were someone cruel or even evil. This does not mean you are doomed to unhappiness in your current life. Karma is not about punishment or judgement – it is about letting go of negative mindsets and behaviour, discovering empathy and compassion for yourself and others, and looking ahead to better choices.

Understanding the 'why' behind problems you may be facing will bring you clarity. Knowing you have found the inception or root of these offers you momentum and reminds you that you – and only you – have control over your thoughts, intentions, words and deeds.

Once you have viewed your past lives and understood how they have brought you to the point you are at now, you simply let them go or decide to rewrite past-life history by visualizing or writing it down. Just return in your mind to that past-life scenario and rescript the outcome, so there is always an empowering happy ending. For example, if you were born to a life of servitude, you can rewrite your past so you escape slavery and claim your freedom. If you had dysfunctional marriages, you can rewrite the past so you either leave that marriage and find someone who treats you with respect, or find ways to communicate better and have compassion for each other.

And if your past Records choose to spotlight your past in this current life, you can apply the same rewriting technique. You can also mentally travel back in time and be there for yourself. For example, if you had a traumatic and lonely childhood, you could visit your childhood self and provide the comfort, parenting and unconditional love you needed but didn't get.

## Present Records

Viewing your past Records can help you understand, release and mend any unresolved conflict. Although this is incredibly therapeutic, asking to view your current records may be even more healing. They can reveal your present situation from a different perspective and help you see clearly what kind of energy your current mindset, behaviour and actions are attracting. You can then use this information to raise your soul's energy vibration by focusing less on what is negative and more on what is positive.

Present Record work can also show you things in your current situation that you may have overlooked, but which your soul wants you to heed. For example, you may see images of your children's downcast eyes and you answering a work call during a family dinner. Indeed, any impression from your present Records will show how every choice you make imprints its energy on the Records and from there sets a potential future in motion.

HUNOLT
PREDIG
III THEIL
R.P. CALINI
SERMONES
TOMUS.I
R.P. CALINI
SERMONES
TOMUS.II

## FUTURE VIEWING

Here are some suggested steps for seeing a potential future in an Akashic reading. First, decide what question you have about your future and what area of your life it will focus on. Then ask the Records how that future might play out. My advice would be to start your future readings with more general requests. For example, you may ask what your life will look in a year from now.

Then find somewhere calm and safe, sit comfortably and close your eyes. Take some deep breaths, focus your attention on opening your heart and release any expectations or judgement. Perform your chosen Akashic pathway. When access is given, ask to see the Book of Your Future – visualize it as a book, computer screen or in other ways. Whenever images or sensations start flowing in, notice them. Remain a calm and objective observer.

If you don't understand what is revealed, trust you are receiving the information for a good reason. You can call on your guides and helpers if there are things you need to see or know and to find out if there is anything you should change in your current life to increase your chances of a welcome future. If you meet your future self in the Records, send yourself endless love across time and ask what your future self wants to tell you about your current life.

When the timing feels right, thank your guides and the Records and close your reading. Immediately write down in your Akashic readings journal any impressions about your future potential that you experienced.

## Future Records

You may view information from your future in a reading and this is always illuminating. However, it is only ever a potential future, as it is based on your current behaviour. As soon as you change this, another potential future will be revealed.

If you glimpse a future in a reading you're unhappy with, you are not predestined to live it. Altering your future is always a choice you can make in the present by changing your current thoughts, feelings, words and actions, and that is why you should view your future Records as often as you can. You need to believe in, feel at peace with, and fall in love with the future direction of your life before it happens. You need to believe it before you see it.

## Future forward

If your future Akashic readings don't impress you, or make you feel uncomfortable, remember the familiar Akashic refrain: you can change your future by changing your present choices. Indeed, helping you make changes in the present that are more in the direction of your soul's evolution is the point of a future reading.

You can improve the clarity and quality of your Akashic future life readings by spending time outside your reading visualizing or thinking about the kind of future you want to see.

Create and then believe in a happy future for yourself and imagine that happy future imprinting itself on the Book of Your Life. In your mind, visit that happy future repeatedly. This will help energetically programme your future Records. During the day, if you have any lingering doubts about yourself and your future potential, return in your mind and heart to this happy depiction of your future that already exists and is simply waiting to be lived.

# Asking about world events

When you've done readings for yourself and feel more confident with Akashic Record work, you may want to do a reading to help you better understand the meaning of world events, the reasons behind them and potential future outcomes – such as a war, political situation or natural or man-made disaster.

As for a personal reading, the best place to start is with calmness, respect and an open mind. Make sure your question follows the same question guidelines outlined on pages 155–158 and decide in advance whether you want to visit the past, present or future timeline. Notice whatever impressions come through, close your reading with gratitude and write those insights down. Then use your intuition to brainstorm those insights to see if they can bring you greater understanding.

Be sure to date your reading, especially if you ask for a potential future reading, because should that future ever play out, you need proof that you are a visionary.

# Go on, impress yourself

Consider how your present life is going to be viewed one day as a past life. Any information that surfaces in a reading, whether past-, present- or future-focused, should always be used to help you become more conscious of your current behaviour and whether it is benefitting your future self. Let go of fear and anxiety and any repeating tension that might imprint itself on your future potential.

Akashic Record work will make you more conscious of your thoughts and actions. You will step back and ask yourself questions such as:

- Am I choosing to be optimistic, compassionate, honest and happy?
- Am I being authentic or am I losing myself due to chasing validation from others?
- Am I learning and growing from every challenge, mistake or setback?
- Am I being as kind as possible to myself and others?
- Am I repeating self-defeating mindsets, relationships, situations and associations, or opening my mind to new horizons?
- Am I choosing doubt and fear, or letting in love and joy?
- Are my thoughts and feelings managing me, or am I managing them?

Think, feel and do everything you can right now in this present moment to impress your future self and choose to live your very best Akashic life. If your life was a TV series and you were the script writer, what would the next episode reveal? You are the script writer, producer and director, the camera crew and the actors in the gripping story of your soul and what happens next is all down to you. The power lies in your choices.

Take a beat now and an Akashic overview of your life. Consider what is being recorded in this very moment about you and whether you would like to watch it again in a past-life reading. Then aim ever higher and higher and consider the story of your soul as belonging to the Akashic library or record collection of every soul and everything. What energy vibration are you contributing to others, to the world and to the cosmos?

# Living your best Akashic life

✦

The end of this book is near, but remember the Book of Your Life has opened its contents to you and your story will never end.

I hope what you have discovered has helped you become aware of your own infinite potential. Working with your Akashic Records can help you figure out that the journey of your soul has no destination. It is all about the journey and your ongoing process of higher self-awareness.

Akashic Record work can help you live in a place of trust and release the need to be perfect or to control outcomes. Trying to seek validation from outward circumstances, or the things in life that you have no control over, is a never-ending recipe for unhappiness. You only need to focus on what you can control, which is yourself and your choices.

Taking an objective, observational and infinitely loving look at your life and viewing it as endless – spanning your past, present and potential future and beyond – can give you a tremendous sense of liberation and inner empowerment. It can also give you a deep sense of purpose, but not in the sense you might think.

A sense of purpose is good for your holistic well-being, but worrying too much about this can have the opposite effect. Your purpose is to become your higher true self and connect with your soul. You are not here to talk about your purpose or waste energy worrying what that purpose is. You are here to live your best human life, to learn how to transcend negative energy and/or karma in this life and become your higher self. You are here to grow in self-awareness through all the changes of your life, to let go of negative patterns and to consciously choose love for yourself and others. You are here – in the words of the famous Serenity Prayer – to embody the serenity of accepting the things you cannot change, and the courage to change the things you can and the wisdom to know the difference.

Your purpose is to take responsibility for your own inner peace. This is the mission of your soul and all you need to do is to choose to accept it.

Moving forward, whenever life gets tough, or you feel you have lost your sense of meaning, doing an Akashic Record reading can remind you that you're so much more than your body and even your mind. You are not a victim of your thoughts, feelings and external circumstances and you can always rise above to the Akashic Realm and choose how you react. You can access an infinite timeline that external circumstances can never touch and do so not just in a formal reading, but any time you open your mind and heart to the Records. Whenever you feel called to open your Records, don't hesitate. Your time to read them is always now.

The Akashic Records can help you become aware of yourself and take responsibility for your choices. They can help you recognize time and time again that what happens to you is of no consequence. Everything that is imprinted in your Records hinges on how you react in the moment and the choices you make with your thoughts, feelings and actions.

You have within you all the resources you need to access and bring Akashic Record inspiration into your life. The Records are a limitless source of healing, guidance and love and your peaceful refuge from the confusion and illusion of life. They are an ongoing reminder that you're a fallible human being but also a light being, and regularly tuning into your inner light and knowing can help you transcend any change and challenge in your life. Every Akashic reading you do can help you foster the self-awareness, self-love and self-belief your inner light needs to spiral higher and higher and shine forever stronger and brighter.

The Akashic Records are always there to help you recognize the infinite light, love and endless wisdom of your own soul.

*Say it out loud: My Akashic Records are always there for me to recognize the infinite light, love and endless wisdom of my own soul.*

## YOUR PURPOSE, ON PURPOSE

Your purpose is to evolve and find meaning in the process of self-realization, which means the fulfilment of your soul's potential. Let's unpick this here.

Every single experience in your life is a lesson, but don't interpret this to mean that once you've learned something about yourself, then you have control over the situation or circumstance. You will be wiser, but control over circumstances is an illusion. Anything you discover about yourself from your time in the Records is more about acquiring self-knowledge or self-realization, as well as learning that your reaction is always more important than any given life situation.

In other words, knowing yourself intimately and, instead of reacting to life's experiences, viewing them through the loving and wise lens of your higher self. Instead of blaming, hating or feeling guilty when things don't go your way, you take responsibility for yourself and take your power back. You see everyone and everything, yourself included, from a higher perspective. You are no longer a victim of your life but a creator of it.

# No going back now

It is often said that a mind stretched by a new experience can never return to its old dimension. Well, your mind has not just been stretched by the Akashic Record reading wisdom shared in this book, it has also expanded beyond measure. It has been unleashed.

There truly is no going back. What you have discovered about yourself here cannot ever be unlearned or tethered. It has become imprinted in the Book of Your Life. From now on, for you, dear visionary reader, it is forever going to be onwards and upwards!

Say it out loud:

*My Infinite Akashic Wisdom is Unleashed.*

*I have the power to choose, create and attract the blissful life my soul desires.*

# INDEX

**A**
affirmations 109–10, 111
Akashic Records 10–11, 28 *see also* pathways
  accessing 12, 14, 18, 20–1, 36
  benefits of 50–1
  closing 153–4
  discerning 71
  for everyone 13
  and fear 159
  history 31–4
  misconceptions about 12–19
  and near-death experiences 12
  and personal growth 14, 16, 47
  physical manifestation 27
  and predicting the future 17
  preparing for readings 61–73
  reality of 17
  relaxing into 14
  and religion 18, 32–3
  searching 153–63
  and self-healing 20
  and self-reflection 18
  substance of 29–30
Angels 20, 53–4, 57, 166–7
animal guides 57
anxiety 14, 86, 161
aphantasia 79
astrology 139
aura 92
automatic writing 130

**B**
base chakra 92
bibliomancy 139
Book of Your Life *see* Akashic Records
books *see* bibliomancy
Buddha & Buddhism 32, 42, 56

**C**
Capra, Fritjof 37–8
Cayce, Edgar 34, 44
celebrities 57
chakras 48, 90–100
  balancing 92–3, 95
  case study 96–7
  *Chakra Exercise* 98–100
  *Chakra Scan Exercise* 95
  and crystals 146
  and intuition 129
  seven major chakras 92–3
  soul star chakra 94–5
channelling 20, 49, 50
Christ & Christianity 32, 56
clairaudience 69
claircognizance 69
clairsentience 69
clairvoyance 69
cloud-watching 87
collective consciousness 35, 37–8
collective energy 18, 29–30, 35, 37–8, 87
consciousness 20, 27, 32
  collective 35, 37–8
  higher 36
  science of 37–8
creativity 46
crown chakra 93
crystals 143–9
  case study 148
  choosing 144–6
  preparing and using 146–7

**D**
daydreaming 69, 86, 126, 160
death: near-death experiences 12
Departed Loved Ones 56
Dickens, Charles *A Christmas Carol* 174
discernment 71
divination 17
dreaming 22, 115–26 *see also* daydreaming
case study 119
and crystals 143
decoding dreams 124–6
and essential oils 143
and intuition 129
liminal states 125
napping 125
nightmares 117, 125
power of 116–17
precognitive 118
psychic dreams 118
recall and tracking 122–3

**E**
Egypt, Ancient 31
Ehrmann, Max *Desiderata* 112
Einstein, Albert 41
energy *see also* chakras
blockages 96–7
collective 18, 29–30, 37–8, 87
continuous nature of 40
negative 161
personal 9, 10, 17, 18, 35, 42, 49, 50, 85
transformative 57
energy vibrations 10, 18, 35
enlightenment 29, 42
essential oils 143
ether 10, 29
etheric Akash plane 10
experience 13

**F**
fear 28, 159, 161
fortune-telling 141
the future 10, 17, 44–6, 178–9

**G**
gazing 86
gratitude 65, 105
grounding 65, 105, 154
growth, personal 14, 181, 182–3, 184
guides 13, 20, 53–4
Angels 20, 53–4, 57
animal guides 57
awareness of 58
Departed Loved Ones 56, 166
famous people 57
guidance from 165, 169–70
higher self 57, 171–2
Lords of the Records 20, 55
Masters 20, 56, 166
prayers to 107–8
teachers 13, 20, 53–4, 56

**H**
heart chakra 93
higher self 57, 171–2, 182
Hinduism 10, 18, 42
hope 46
Howe, Linda 105
human design 140

**I**
*I Ching* 140
India, Ancient 31
intentions 64, 77, 94, 95, 120
intuition 16, 22, 48, 49, 66, 68–9, 128–41
astrology 139
automatic writing 130
bibliomancy 139
case study 132

crystals 143–9
empowering 131
and essential oils 143
human design 140
*I Ching* 140
numerology 140–1
runes 141
scrying 141
Tarot cards 133–8
tea-leaf reading 141
vs wisdom 128
Islam 32

J
journalling 62, 70, 84, 115, 118, 122–3, 129, 154
Judaism 32–3
judgement 28

K
karma 42, 47, 175
Krishna 56

L
liminal states 125
Lords of the Records 20, 55
love, unconditional 46, 54, 57, 58

M
mantras 110, 111
Masters 20, 56, 166
Mayans 32
meditation 49, 61, 66, 77, 129
*A 20-Minute Guided Akashic Meditation* 80–3
*Asking Your Akashic Guide for Help* 169–70
case study 85
*First Akashic Record Reading Meditation* 78–9
gazing 86
looking into your own eyes 88
and nature 87–8
role of music & dance 86
and visualization 79, 86
*Wisdom of the Heart Meditation* 67
Metatron (Angel) 32–3, 167
mindset, changing 17, 40, 44, 125
Mohammed 56
morphic resonance 35
music 86

N
near-death experiences (NDEs) 12
negative impulses 14
negative thinking 44–5, 71, 109
nightmares 117, 125
Nostradamus 33
numerology 140–1

O
the Observer Effect 45
the 'occult' 16
opposites, embracing 18

P
palm leaf reading 31
parallel universes 38
the past 36, 40–1, 42
past-life records 175–6
rewriting 43, 176
pathways 20–1, 72–3 *see also* chakras; crystals; dreaming; intuition; meditation; prayer
people
engaging with 87–8
searching records for 162
positive thinking 44–5, 104, 109
prayer 18, 102–13, 129
affirmations 109–10, 111
case study 112–13
mantras 110, 111

*Pathway Prayer* 105
suggestions 106, 107–8
for yourself 104
preparing for Akashic readings 61–73
discernment 71
environment 62
grounding and gratitude 65
intuition 66, 68–9
journalling 70
meditation and relaxation 61–2, 66–7
physical comfort 64
timing and planning 64–5
the present 42, 44, 176, 181
psychic ability 16

## Q

quantum physics 37–8
questions, asking 155–8, 163

## R

reincarnation 20, 40–1, 175
relaxation 62
religion and Akashic Records 18, 32–3
resistance 28
runes 141

## S

sacral chakra 92
science of consciousness 37–8
scrying 141
searching Akashic Records 153–63
asking questions 155–8, 163
and fear 159, 161
finding nothing 160
and negative energies 161
for someone else 162
self-awareness 14, 16, 18, 46, 84, 126, 182
self-belief 16, 17, 46, 62, 126, 143
self-esteem 13
self-healing 20
self-knowledge 16, 140, 184
self-love 46, 85, 126, 143
self-reflection 18, 28
Sheldrake, Rupert 35
sleep, importance of 116
solar plexus chakra 93, 96–7
the soul 29, 36
soul star chakra 94–5
star-gazing 87
Steiner, Rudolf 34

## T

Tarot cards 133–8
Major Arcana 133–7
Minor Arcana 133, 137
case study 132
*Three-Card Reading* 138
tea-leaf reading 141
teachers 13, 20, 53–4, 56
third eye chakra 93
throat chakra 93
time *see* the future; the past
timelines
eternal 41
linear 153, 156
trance state 12

## V

visualization 23, 44–6, 79, 86
*A 20-Minute Guided Akashic Meditation* 80–3
*First Akashic Record Reading Meditation* 78–9

## W

weaknesses 14
Western culture 33–4
wisdom 67, 71, 128
world events 180

# SUGGESTED FURTHER READING

### AUTHOR DETAILS

www.theresacheung.com
Instagram @thetheresacheung
Author pages on X and Facebook
Reader email for asking questions and sharing Akashic stories: angeltalk710@aol.com
My *White Shores* podcast is available on all free podcast platforms.

### AKASHIC WEBSITES

Edgar Cayce's A.R.E.: https://edgarcayce.org/
Edgar Cayce on the Akashic Records:
https://www.edgarcayce.org/the-readings/akashic-records/
Akashic Records Institute:
https://www.akashicrecordsinstitute.com/history-akashic-records/

### FURTHER READING

Brian Weiss, *Many Lives, Many Masters*
Ervin Laszlo, *The Self-Actualizing Cosmos: The Akasha Revolution in Science and Human Consciousness*
Georgia Coleridge, *The Chakra Project: How the Healing Power of Energy Can Transform Your Life*
Linda Howe, *How To Read The Akashic Records: Accessing the Archive of the Soul and Its Journey*
Masaru Emoto, *The Hidden Messages in Water*
Michael Newton, *Journey of Souls: Case Studies of Life Between Lives*
Robert Schwartz, *Your Soul's Plan: Discovering the Real Meaning of the Life You Planned Before You Were Born*
Theresa Cheung, *The Dream Dictionary from A to Z: The Ultimate A–Z to Interpret the Secrets of Your Dreams*

There are also many online resources – try YouTube and Insight Timer for Akashic Record meditations and guided visualizations, as well as Akashic chakra work and dreamwork. And search for Akashic Record reading blogs and podcasts, too.

# ACKNOWLEDGEMENTS

The Akashic Records will forever glow with the positive, loving energy of all the people who inspired and worked on this book, and I am eternally grateful.

Thank you to my publishers, Octopus, for their faith in me and to my visionary editor Louisa Johnson. I would also like to thank Lucy Pessell for her support. Sincere gratitude to my copyeditor Caroline West and everyone involved in the production, artwork, distribution and promotion of this book.

I would also like to thank all the scientists, neuroscientists and psychologists I have worked with along the way and the consciousness-raising vibrations of all the experts I have interviewed (and will continue to interview) on my *White Shores* podcast. Special thanks to Gail Torr for being a dream to work with and to my agent Mark Gottlieb at Trident Media Group for smoothing the way ahead.

Heartfelt thanks to my family. I could not have written this book without your love and my soul dog, Arnie, for forever being by my side.

Most important of all are my readers and listeners. You are a constant source of inspiration and joy to me. I'm fully aware you are all busy recording your own Akashic Records and I feel deeply honoured whenever you set aside some of your precious time to read or listen to me. Thank you from my heart and soul.